THREE MIDWEST
HISTORY PLAYS

. . . and then some

HANK FINCKEN

*Frank,
what would
we have done w/o you? I
am so pleased to have you as a
friend. We have shared great moments
together this summer. I am forever grateful.
Hail Fred
July 17, 2002*

Guild Press of Indiana

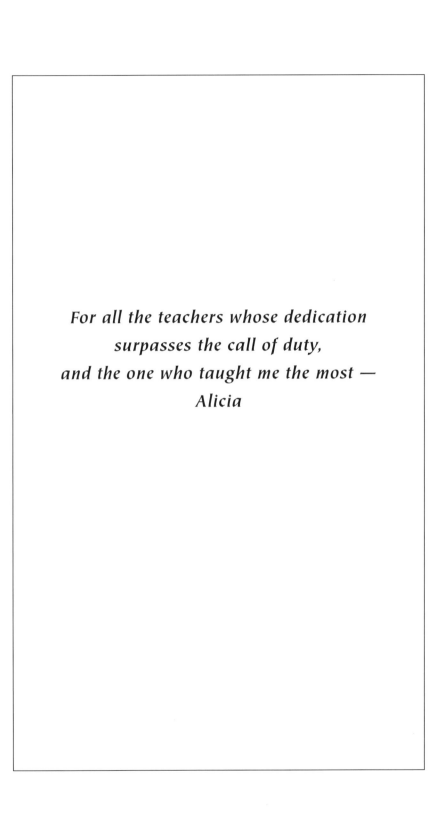

For all the teachers whose dedication
surpasses the call of duty,
and the one who taught me the most —
Alicia

TABLE OF CONTENTS

Acknowledgments

I WOULD LIKE TO EXPRESS MY APPRECIATION to two Indiana authors for permitting me to use their works for the basis of two of the plays in this book:

Thanks to Nancy Niblack Baxter, whose book *The Miamis!* (Guild Press of Indiana, 1987) was the basis for "The Way of the Spirit Bird."

Lucina Ball Moxley's book *The Mexican Dollhouse* (Guild Press of Indiana, 1996), the third book in her Dandy Dollhouse Stories series, was the inspiration for "Doll Sense."

I would also like to thank the Indiana Arts Commission for their grants which enabled me to work at Royerton Elementary School in Muncie, Indiana. The early drafts of "The Clark Campaign," "One Good Turn," and "The History Lesson" were first produced there.

"The Clark Campaign" first appeared in *The Indiana Junior Historian*, published by the Indiana Historical Bureau, in January 1991.

Hank Fincken
February 1998

Introduction

SINCE BEFORE THE TIME OF THE GREEKS, theatre has been a team sport. For those teachers and students who tackle these plays, I promise you will experience joy, frustration, anger, delight, and new insight into our own Midwest heritage. Each play offers a unique challenge. None is easy. All offer an opportunity for personal growth and cultural understanding. In theatre, no one has to lose.

The history plays do not lend themselves to simple interpretations. The research I did demanded that each play attempt to recapture the complexity of the past. I want the audience to appreciate the struggles our ancestors experienced so we can better understand our own struggles today. Even if we disagree about solutions, we can share a common understanding of the questions.

The non-history plays should be fun, but in their own way thought-provoking. Sometimes the most revolutionary ideas are camouflaged in comedy. Laughter helps us drop our defenses and listen to ideas we might reject if told in drama or lecture.

I believe that the production of each play will provide a lifetime memory. How can I be sure? Theatre teaches tolerance (literally standing in another's shoes), cooperation, self-confidence, and commitment to an ideal. It's learning through experience (rather than passive sitting), and it allows students a positive outlet for all that energy that drives the classroom teacher crazy.

I have thoroughly enjoyed writing these plays. Part of my joy has been the anticipation of your pleasure as my words take on new life and characters grow beyond my expectations. That is why I love my work. You and I are working together—even if we never meet. As I said: Theatre is a team sport. We make each other look good!

Hank Fincken
February 1998

THE WAY OF THE SPIRIT BIRD

Based on the book THE MIAMIS *by Nancy Niblack Baxter*

IN 1810 A MEETING OF THE MIAMI CLANS—similar to what happens in this play—did occur. Though the discussion was not recorded, the dilemma behind all the talk remains clear: should the Miami join Tecumseh in an all-out war with the whites or should they follow Little Turtle and continue living in peace?

If this play had been set in 1790, the Miami would have decided quickly and easily: war! But twenty years of experience had taught leaders such as Little Turtle that victory was unlikely. A good spirit and proper commitment were not enough. General "Mad" Anthony Wayne had proved as thoughtful a fighter as he was disciplined. The Americans had an infinite supply of men and better weapons.

But Tecumseh's plan made sense: If all the Indian nations united, they would be more powerful than any American army. The memories of better times and broken treaties made peace seem unpalatable. This might be the last chance for the native people to defeat the invader. In addition, Tecumseh's brother, Tenskwatawa, the Prophet, had had a vision: Because their cause was just, the Great Spirit promised to protect them from all harm.

The four stories told at the campfire are based on Miami myths. If I have taken liberties with these stories, please remember: the energy of the original stories in their own language in their own time is dulled by a loss of cultural reference points and translation. My task as playwright is to be true to the spirit of the story and recapture the energy that delighted audiences in 1810.

CAST: For the Miami, war was always a community decision (including women). Therefore, at least two clan leaders should be played by girls (Chief 3 and Stone Eater). Because they eventually left their tribe to fight with Tecumseh, we know the names of certain chiefs: Loon, Catfish, and Stone Eater. A-son-da-ki, is a composite character, who was first introduced in Nancy Niblack Baxter's novel *The Movers*. In this play he is Tecumseh's chief spokesman. Chiefs 1–4 all favor Little Turtle. Since their names are not recorded, the actors are encouraged to invent their own Indian names. Eventually, there will be eight clan leaders on stage, two more in the front row of the audience, and the Meda priest. Because he is older and wiser (and the only member of the cast played by an adult), he is called Uncle. The audience needs to be advised in advance of its role as silent clan leaders.

If the production is an in-class project, the animals can be played by other members of the class. If the production is for the public, then Chiefs 9 and 10 should play the roles as described in this script.

COSTUMES: For this play, I recommend that the clan leaders wear a symbolic piece of Indian attire over a simple costume of jeans and colored T-shirts. This piece—be it headdress, bracelet, leggings, or war apparel should stand out. I hope that this symbolic representation of Indian dress will create a bond between the past and present and keep the cost of production low. Uncle should be dressed in full native attire.

Likewise, the animals (Bear, Deer, etc.) might also wear symbolic costume pieces to help the audience distinguish who is who. For example, Buffalo might have a two-horn head piece, Bear a robe, and Elm might stand on a log.

SETTING: The stage is empty except for a camp fire (electric) in the upper center stage area. This fire should produce light and contain a flashlight-torch and a log (cut to easily break during performance). Other props include a stick, a bow, arrows, and an ax. Two clan leaders enter with the audience and sit in the front row. When the other eight enter, they sit upstage of the fire in a half circle. Most of the acting will be done downstage of the fire. A black curtain, representing a late fall evening, can serve as a backdrop.

Vocabulary

The following words should be reviewed with the audience before the play begins so they will know their meaning.

Ke-ki-on-ga .... The Miami home village at Fort Wayne, Indiana.

sassafras .... Tree whose dried bark was used for a medicinal tea.

Meda priest .... One who communicates with the Great Spirit and Manittos.

Mos-wa .... Deer

We-mi-am-iki .... The Miami, "All Beavers," or good folk

Mississinewa .... River in central Indiana where the Miami lived.

Long Knives .... Indian term for the white soldiers.

Manittos .... Indian Spirit Gods

Tecumseh .... A great Shawnee Indian chief

Little Turtle .... The great chief of the Miami (Me-shi-kin-o-qua)

Governor Harrison . The Indiana governor who later became the 9th President of the United States.

It is an early evening in the fall of 1810.

[The curtain is open when the audience enters. When the audience is settled, the Meda priest enters, stokes the fire, and then seems surprised to find the audience.]

UNCLE   Ah! You are skilled travelers, quieter than Mos-wa. I did not hear you arrive. I trust your journey was safe and that you completed the harvest before you left your homes. These are difficult times and I know it was a sacrifice to come. I thank you. Your wisdom and council are most welcome.

[Offstage noises of people greeting each other.]

Good! The others have arrived. Please allow me to make one suggestion. Listen closely to what is said tonight, weigh the consequences of each opinion carefully, and then decide what is best—not for you or your clan—but the whole Miami nation. The future is tonight. Choose quickly but not in haste. Let the wisdom of the Spirit Bird be your guide.

[The eight enter in twos and threes. It is obvious that some are very happy to see each other. Others treat their peers with polite reservation. When all are seated, there is an uncomfortable pause: something is not right.]

CHIEF 2   Uncle, where are Little Turtle and Tecumseh? We came to hear them speak.

UNCLE   They have been delayed. I hope they will be here soon.

A-SON-DA-KI   *[standing and crossing downstage]* I can speak for Tecumseh. I have shared bread with him many times and know his thoughts.

CHIEF 1   *[crossing downstage to Chief 5, a mild confrontation]* And I know Little Turtle's. We could save much time if I share the wisdom of his years.

UNCLE   *[coming between them]* Thank you both. Little Turtle and Tecumseh are lucky to have such worthy speakers represent their ideas, but I suggest we wait for their arrival and thus avoid any misunderstandings. Besides, your journey has been long and tiring. You must clear your heads of all negative thoughts before we begin the debate. Tonight, we must all be alert and wise like the Mississinewa.

[During this talk, Uncle escorts the two leaders to their seats.]

LOON   How can a river be wise, Uncle, if it is always running at the mouth?

UNCLE   Ah, but listen to what it says. The river has learned how to survive the worst droughts and floods. If we are to survive as a nation, then tonight we must be river wise.

A-SON-DA-KI   Uncle, you imply that all things old are wise. I disagree. Some gain wisdom through time but others lose it. The stagnant pond collects muck, not wisdom. It may last forever but for what purpose? I would not want our Miami nation to become a stagnant pond.

CHIEF 3   Uncle, I have an idea. While we wait and to clear our minds, let us tell stories we learned in our youth. To make them appropriate, each tale should reveal a lesson that might guide our discussion tonight.

A-SON-DA-KI   A lesson can come from one who succeeds or one who fails. Faulty reasoning and cowardice instruct in the same way wisdom and bravery inspire.

UNCLE   Excellent idea, ———(3). The past should always enlighten the present. . . . All right, who wants to start? Who remembers a story that somehow reflects the Spirit Bird's wisdom and will leave us with food for thought.

CHIEF 4   The Spirit Bird says we should outthink our enemies. What better example than the western story of Coyote.

[Because there are many stories about Coyote, there is some disagreement.]

CHIEF 2   Coyote?

CATFISH   Coyote thinks quickly because he thinks with his stomach.

CHIEF 3   In that he is like you, Catfish.

CATFISH   A full stomach is a sign of clear thinking.

CHIEF 1   Or selfishness!

LOON   I admire Coyote because he uses his nose like a second pair of eyes.

STONE EATER   If he sees twice as much, he should make half the mistakes.

CHIEF 4   Stop! You are all forgetting how Coyote brought us fire.

UNCLE   Tell us ———(4). Remind us how Coyote used his wits to bring us fire.

[Chief 4 Crosses downstage and picks Chief 9 to be Coyote and

Chief 10 to be Sis-nin-i-koo. While he talks, he appoints Chief 2 to be Snake, Stone Eater to be Lion, and Catfish to be Bear. While the telling of these stories is serious, it should be equally obvious the actors are having a good time, in marked contrast to the war debate. The actors need to add gestures and movement to make their animal characters clear. When the animals are all in position—Snake, then Mountain Lion, then Bear, then Sis-nin-i-koo sitting by the fire. Chief 4 crosses downstage right to act as narrator.]

CHIEF 4   A long time ago, the world was warm and there was little need of fire. Fruits and vegetables grew everywhere and clothing was strictly a decoration. Then the world cooled, people shivered, and fewer plants grew. Suddenly, fire was not just a luxury occasionally supplied by lightning but a necessity for everyday survival. Because fire was so dangerous, the Manittos kept it hidden deep in the earth, with Snake, Mountain Lion, Bear, and the great magician Sis-nin-i-koo standing guard. In those days, the We-mi-am-iki were very shy . . .

A-SON-DA-KI   *[Interrupting]* Shy or cowardly?

UNCLE   Shh! Let ———(4) tell the story.

CHIEF 4   They decided the best way to get fire was to convince Coyote to get it for them.

[At this point, Coyote passes by the seated chiefs who shake his hand and wish him well.]

LOON   Good luck, Coyote. We have every confidence in you.

CHIEF 3   Don't let us down. We're counting on you.

CHIEF 1   If you need any help, just holler. We'll be around here . . . someplace.

CHIEF 4   Coyote traveled deep into the earth, stepping carefully because it was too dark to see. When he came to the first door, he knocked politely . . .

[At this point, the actors take over. Snake sneaks up on Coyote from the other side and scares him to death.]

SNAKE   *[After hissing his greeting]* Coyote, I am surprised to see you here. The Manittos say you are smart, but it cannot be true if you come to take fire away from me.

COYOTE   I mean you no harm, Snake. I just came to borrow it.

SNAKE   Do you take me for a fool? You can't borrow fire. Either you have it or you don't. The Manittos said you are not to have it.

COYOTE   I think they said I have to earn it.

SNAKE   How can you earn it? Hard work? Trickery?

COYOTE   I could never trick you, Snake. You're too smart for that.

SNAKE   I also have these fangs and orders to use them against anyone who tries to "borrow" fire.

COYOTE   Is that all?

SNAKE   [Insulted] What do you mean, "Is that all"? There's enough poison in each fang to kill a pack of mangy coyotes or a tribe of quivering Miami.

[At this point, Snake turns towards the sitting chiefs who jump.]

COYOTE   [While offering his arm.] Big Deal. Any animal could bite through this soft flesh—even the tiny mosquito. If the Manittos left you to protect fire from the likes of me, then they see you as just a big bug.

SNAKE   [Very insulted.] Not so! These fangs are long and sharp. I can bite through anything.

[Coyote reaches down and picks up a stick.]

COYOTE   Even this?

SNAKE   Easily!

COYOTE   [Holding the stick up] I don't believe it.

[Snake clamps down hard on the stick and then realizes he has been tricked. His fangs are buried deep in the wood and he is unarmed (pun intended!). He wiggles off, mumbling threats no one is quite able to understand. He returns to being Chief 2 at the fire.]

CHIEF 4   Coyote was now free to go to the second door, guarded by Mountain Lion.

[Coyote knocks gently on invisible door and Mountain Lion opens it with a roar.]

MOUNTAIN LION Coyote, what are you doing here? Don't you know I have orders to kill anyone who tries to steal fire?

COYOTE I was hoping to earn it.

MOUNTAIN LION How? Hard work, trickery, or would you fight me for it?

COYOTE I'd love to fight you, Mountain Lion, but you wouldn't stand a chance.

MOUNTAIN LION I wouldn't stand a chance? Look at this.

[Mountain Lion picks up a log and snaps it in two.]

MOUNTAIN LION Come on, Coyote. I am ready for you.

COYOTE No. The Spirit Bird says we should always fight fairly and it's against my convictions to take advantage of your weakness.

MOUNTAIN LION [Very insulted] Go ahead; take advantage. I dare you.

COYOTE I'll tell you what. If you can prove yourself a worthy opponent, then I'll fight you.

MOUNTAIN LION How? What do I have to do?

COYOTE Fight Bear, who is just on the other side of that door.

MOUNTAIN LION With pleasure!

[Mountain Lion pounds on the door and then pounces on Bear. The two fight furiously on the floor, rolling over several times, snarling and biting. Finally Bear stops moving and Mountain Lion sits up.]

CHIEF 4 After a ferocious fight, Mountain Lion won . . .

MOUNTAIN LION Am I worthy?

[Coyote blows on him and he falls over.]

CHIEF 4 [Continuing] . . . but just barely. All the doors were now open and there was nothing to stop Coyote from retrieving fire except the silent magician, Sis-nin-i-koo.

[Sis-nin-i-koo sits by the camp fire as if in a trance. Coyote runs

*over and waves his arms around the magician but the man does
not move.]*

COYOTE   He's sound asleep, the perfect time to "borrow" fire.

*[Coyote grabs a torch from the fire and starts to run offstage. He
takes about four steps when Sis-nin-i-koo raises a hand, freezing
Coyote in his tracks.]*

COYOTE   Then again, what if Sis-nin-i-koo is a light sleeper?

*[Sis-nin-i-koo makes a gesture and Coyote begins to walk back-
wards, reversing his past movements until the torch is back in the
fire. He then stands frozen.]*

COYOTE   Something tells me I should not try to trick or outthink this magician. Very impressive, Sis-nin-i-koo.
Is there anything you cannot do?

SIS-NIN-I-KOO   No.

COYOTE   Can you dim fire?

[With a gesture, Sis-nin-i-koo does.]

COYOTE: Can you make it glow brighter?

[With another gesture, Sis-nin-i-koo makes the fire brighten.]

COYOTE   Tell me, wise Sis-nin-i-koo. Why do the Manittos not
want the We-mi-am-iki to have fire?

SIS-NIN-I-KOO   It is dangerous. They might destroy the world.

COYOTE   But if your magic can make fire brighter or dimmer,
can't it make fire fragile too, so fragile it will go out if
not cared for properly? This would teach the We-mi-
am-iki responsibility and make forest fires unlikely—
a solution that would warm people and Manittos, inside and out.

SIS-NIN-I-KOO   I will consider your idea, Coyote. How do you feel?

COYOTE   Stiff.

SIS-NIN-I-KOO   Good. You have learned your limits. Now go.

[Snaps fingers, thus releasing Coyote from the spell.] Take
the torch, but remember: Fire is no toy. The Manittos
will be mad at us both if the We-mi-am-iki abuse this
opportunity.

[Coyote takes the torch runs through the audience and back on stage. Meanwhile the others have all gone to their positions at the fire.]

CHIEF 4	So thanks to Coyote's cleverness, the Miami obtained fire and, just as importantly, learned responsibility.
CATFISH	You mean they should have learned responsibility. Remember what happened next.
CHIEF 4	Oh, they learned responsibility all right. They just didn't practice it.
UNCLE	I like your story, ———(4). It reminds us that we must use our wits to survive.
A–SON–DA–KI	Yes. In the same way Coyote fooled Snake and Mountain Lion, we will fool the Long Knives.
CHIEF 1	You were not listening, A-son-da-ki. Twenty years ago, the whites were like Snake. Today they are like Sis-nin-i-koo. The Spirit Bird says: know your limits. Coyote knew he was never going to outfight or outthink Sis-nin-i-koo.
STONE EATER	Tecumseh says: know your strengths. If all the tribes join together, we will be strong like . . .
CHIEF 3	Mountain Lion? Please. Strength alone will not ensure our survival. We must use our minds the way Sis-nin-i-koo used magic.
CATFISH	Forget that story. If you want a message that will guide us tonight, remember Nan-a-bush.
A–SON–DA–KI	How could we forget? That was the time the We-mi-am-iki grew careless and almost burned up the world. The Great Spirit took fire back and left it in the protection of the powerful Manitto, Fire-Keeper, and his two daughters.
CATFISH	The people were freezing and Coyote was nowhere to be found.
CHIEF 2	*[Interrupting]* Maybe he moved west to get away from the Long Knives.

UNCLE	Shh! Tell the story, Catfish.

[As Catfish speaks, he sets the scene as Chief 4 did before. Chief 9 will be Nan-a-bush, Chief 10 will be Fire-Keeper, and Chiefs 3 and Stone Eater will be his two daughters.]

CATFISH	The We-mi-am-iki called an emergency meeting, much like this one, and then elected one of their own, Nan-a-bush to go retrieve fire.
CHIEF 1	One of their own? Nan-a-bush's father was the West Wind.
UNCLE	Quiet Please. We can discuss the meaning of the story afterward. Catfish. . .
CATFISH	Since Fire-Keeper was suspicious of every human movement, Nan-a-bush decided that the only way to get near fire would be to disguise himself as Rabbit, shivering at the side of the road, just as Fire-Keeper's two daughters passed by.

[Chief 9 is now crouched in the center of the stage, twitching his nose and curling his paws like a rabbit. The two daughters circle the stage and stop several feet away.]

RABBIT/NAN-A-BUSH	*[Sadly]* Here I am all alone: so cold, so hungry, so . . . cute.
DAUGHTER 1	Look, Sis. There's a shivering rabbit all alone at the side of the road—so cold, so hungry, so . . . cute.

[The two run over to cuddle him but Daughter 2 stops suddenly and lifts his arm.]

DAUGHTER 2	My goodness! What happened to his hair?

[Rabbit uses his other arm to wave the hair on his head before batting his eyes.]

DAUGHTER 1	An almost hairless hare.
	[both daughters together, lovingly] Ohhh!
DAUGHTER 2	No wonder he's so cold. Let's take him home.
CATFISH	Together they helped Nan-a-bush home and set him beside the fire.

[After hugging him, the two take Rabbit to the campfire.]

DAUGHTER 1   Don't worry, Rabbit. You'll be warm in no time.

CATFISH   That night when the daughters went to bed . . .

DAUGHTER 2   Good night, you cute, hairless [looks him up and down], oversized Rabbit.

[The two daughters go to bed. Rabbit then stands up, grabs the torch too high, burns himself and drops it.]

RABBIT/NAN-A-BUSH   I've got it! Ouch! No, I don't.

[Fire-Keeper hears the noise and runs to the campfire. Meanwhile, Nan-a-bush returns to being cute Rabbit.]

FIRE-KEEPER   What's going on here? Sheez—what an ugly rabbit!

[He pats the creature on the head and leaves.]

CATFISH   As soon as Fire-Keeper was gone, Rabbit changed back into Nan-a-bush, grabbed the torch correctly, and ran like . . . the wind.

NAN-A-BUSH   [To Catfish] No—the West Wind, my father.

[Nan-a-bush runs into the audience.]

CATFISH   Fire-Keeper returned, saw what had happened, and chased after.

FIRE-KEEPER   [Shouting to daughters] Hey, you two. Your rabbit just stole our fire.

[He runs into the audience, the two daughters close behind. The chase has to be coordinated so that Nan-a-bush is in the center and the others are coming for him from three sides.]

CATFISH   Just as they were about to catch him, Nan-a-bush placed the torch like a tail, and pretended to be Firefly.

[Nan-a-bush holds the torch like a tail, stands up, and makes the sound of a bug. Soon he is bugging everyone.]

FIREFLY/NAN-A-BUSH   [A deep ugly sound] Buzzzz. Buzzzz.

DAUGHTER 1   What is that?

DAUGHTER 2   A big ugly Firefly!

FIREFLY/NAN-A-BUSH   Buzzzz. Buzzzz.

FIRE-KEEPER   [Grabbing the hair on Firefly's head] Sheez, it's even uglier than that hairless Rabbit!

[The three retreat. Firefly makes a small circle through the audience as the others go back to the campfire. When he gets back, Firefly is Nan-a-bush.]

CATFISH   When Nan-a-bush returned home, he was treated as a hero.

[All the chiefs congratulate Nan-a-bush, who then returns to his seat as Chief 9.]

CATFISH   The We-mi-am-iki promised the Great Spirit that this time they would be more responsible and they have kept their word till this day.

UNCLE   Thank you, Catfish. Your story reminds us all that . . .

A-SON-DA-KI   *[Interrupting]* . . . if we want to solve the problem with the Long Knives, we must do it ourselves.

CHIEF 2   But Nan-a-bush didn't. He relied on magic first to disguise himself as Rabbit, then Firefly. If we count on magic to defeat the whites, we will die.

STONE EATER   But we have a potent magic. Tecumseh's brother, the Prophet, has had holy visions. He says The Great Spirit believes in our cause and will let nothing happen to us.

CHIEF 1   Bullets have no respect for magic or just causes.

UNCLE   Since we are not in total agreement about the meaning of of our two stories, maybe someone would like to tell us what happened next.

LOON   You mean after Nan-a-bush returned with fire and the We-mi-am-iki—all warm and well fed—came to believe they were the Great Spirit's favorite?

UNCLE   Exactly. Now you tell the story while I go see what has happened to Tecumseh and Little Turtle.

[Uncle leaves and Loon assigns roles as did the other storytellers. Chief 2 will be Deer, A-son-da-ki will be Bear, Chief 9 will be Buffalo, and Chief 10 will be Possum.]

LOON   The We-mi-am-iki were so pleased with themselves and fire that they grew cruel and killed their animal brothers and sisters beyond need. It was as if they were swatting fleas.

[Loon slaps himself on the arm.]

CHIEF 3   [In a high voice as Flea] Hey, I resent that!

[Loon reaches down and picks up an invisible Flea.]

LOON   [To Flea on fingertip] Of course, Flea. Every creature has its place and importance. The We-mi-am-iki had forgotten that.

[To others] The animals became so afraid, they called a council meeting—much like this one. Bear, Deer, Buffalo, and Possum called the meeting to order.

[The four chiefs have formed a half circle in front of the fire, facing the audience. They move and act like their animal counterparts. Possum is always sleepy. Loon continues to hold Flea on his fingertip.]

BEAR   [In a gruff voice] Thank you all for coming. I know in these times it is dangerous to pass through any land where humans are present.

FLEA/LOON   [In a high voice] Not if you're small. I just hitched a ride on Deer.

POSSUM   To tell the truth, the trip exhausted me. I suggest we all take a nap and decide what to do tomorrow.

[Possum rolls over, but Bear's response wakes him up quickly.]

BEAR   No! We must decide what to do now.

[Buffalo raises his hand.]

BEAR   Buffalo.

BUFFALO   I suggest we move west where the grass is tall and there are no trees to block our view of stalking humans.

DEER   But I like trees. Their shadows serve as protection. Besides, this is my home.

POSSUM   Why don't we just roll over and play dead every time we see them. If we borrow some stink from skunk, they will never touch us again.

[Possum rolls over and plays dead. The other animals huddle around him.]

DEER   You can't play dead forever.

POSSUM   [Still dead] Yes, I can.

BUFFALO   But won't the humans grow suspicious of a talking corpse?

POSSUM   Not if I stink.

[The others are disgusted and move away.]

BEAR   We have no choice. We must declare war on the We-mi-am-iki.

POSSUM   [Sitting up] But the We-mi-am-iki have bows, arrows, and axes.

BEAR   Then we will fight them with bows, arrows, and axes.

LOON   This seemed such a clever idea that all the animals agreed at once.

[The animals cheer and then collect the weapons. As Loon explains the problems the animals had, he passes among them. Possum needs to be next to Deer.]

LOON   Unfortunately, the war with the We-mi-am-iki got off to a poor start. Or more accurately, it never got started. Bear found his claws were too big to use the bow.

BEAR   [After twanging himself] Ouch!

LOON   And Buffalo nearly shot himself in the foot.

[Buffalo drops an arrow and then starts hopping up and down as if it hit his foot.]

LOON   Deer, whose arms and legs are perfect for sprinting, could never get a good grip on ax.

[Deer attempts to throw the ax, but it drops behind him, crashing beside Possum, who immediately yells "Yipes!" and rolls over and plays dead.]

LOON   Bear decided to call a second meeting.

[While the others take their positions as before, Possum collects the dropped weapons as if getting ready for battle.]

BEAR   I'm afraid the war with the We-mi-am-iki goes badly.
              All of our brothers and sisters are wounded, and we
              have yet to meet the enemy.

[Possum comes up behind Bear.]

POSSUM   Charge!

*[The animals scream and run to hide in the audience. The scream
scares Possum who drops the weapons, rolls over, and plays
dead.]*

POSSUM   Yipes!

[The others slowly and cautiously return to the stage.]

POSSUM   *[Still dead]* Have they left yet?

ALL OTHERS   Yes!

*[Possum goes to his position. The others go to theirs. During the
next sequence, Flea is ignored.]*

BEAR   I don't know what else we can do.

FLEA/LOON   I have an idea.

BUFFALO   I told you we should move west.

FLEA/LOON   I said, I have an idea.

DEER   When we are all gone, the We-mi-am-iki will starve
              to death. Then they'll be sorry!

BEAR   How can they be sorry if they're dead?

FLEA/LOON   Hey, are you all deaf? I said I have an idea!

POSSUM   You? You're not big or strong enough to have an idea.

FLEA/LOON   That's what the We-mi-am-iki say about you.

BEAR   What's your idea?

FLEA/LOON   I will teach them humility. I will teach them how the
              big and the little are equally important to the Great
              Spirit. I will present them to my smaller cousin, Dis-
              ease.

*[All the animals jump back. Possum shouts "Yipes!" again and
rolls over on his back.]*

BUFFALO   Why Disease?

FLEA/LOON   Because little Disease prevents even the mightiest

	from taking himself too seriously.
DEER	How will you do it?
FLEA/LOON	I will talk to Disease; Bear will carry him to Ke-ki-on-ga. Big and little working together. The Manittos will be pleased.

[As Loon concludes the story, the animals again become Miami chiefs and return to their original positions at the campfire.]

LOON	And so, the We-mi-am-iki were reminded how all creatures big and small are equally vulnerable and valuable to the Great Spirit.
CHIEF 2	Learning humility can be very painful.
CHIEF 1	But from humility comes wisdom.
CATFISH	It is too bad the whites were not here when the We-mi-am-iki learned humility. Then they too would apologize before killing Bear, Deer, Buffalo, and Possum.
STONE EATER	The whites also carried Disease. Was that part of Flea's plan to teach us humility?
A-SON-DA-KI	No! Humility is a virtue. The white man wants to teach us humiliation. It is not the same.

[Suddenly Uncle arrives and all discussion stops.]

CHIEF 1	Uncle, what news of Little Turtle?
A-SON-DA-KI	And Tecumseh?
UNCLE	There is no sign of either. Perhaps they were detained by storm.
CHIEF 4	Or the Long Knives.
STONE EATER	No, they are too smart for that.
UNCLE	We will wait a little longer . . . Well, have you decided what was the meaning of Loon's story?
A-SON-DA-KI	The message is obvious. To defeat the whites, we must unite as one, the same as Bear, Deer, Buffalo, and Flea. Together we will surprise them with our strength.
CHIEF 2	No. The message is the opposite. Bows, arrows, and

axes will no more serve us than they did the animals. We are outnumbered and outarmed whatever we do. That is why we must heed the Spirit Bird's warning and make a peace that will last for eternity.

[The others begin to protest when Chief 1 interrupts.]

CHIEF 1   Wait! The story is not over. For Loon's tale to mean anything tonight, he must tell of Chipmunk's role in limiting the power of Disease.

[Several chiefs laugh.]

LOON   Chipmunk? Chipmunk is always too busy playing to be of any service. He is certainly no Meda Priest like you, Uncle.

CHIEF 1   I never claimed he was a priest, just a friend.

UNCLE   Remind us, ———(1). Tell us again of Chipmunk's service.

CHIEF 1   Disease did not just teach the We-mi-am-iki humility. It also destroyed their pride. Since they could not fight this enemy with bows, arrows, or axes, our people gave up. They needed a friend, an outsider, to fight this battle for them.

LOON   Chipmunk is no fighter. How could he stop Disease?

UNCLE   That's the story, Loon. Let ———(1) tell it.

[Chief 1 narrates the story as the others did before him. Chief 9 will be Chipmunk, Chief 10 will be Sassafras, and Uncle will be mighty Elm, standing on a log or box.]

CHIEF 1   As you all know, Chipmunk has always been a friend of the We-mi-am-iki. What you have forgotten is that while he seems to be playing, he is really watching out for us. When Disease turned human pride into corn mush, Chipmunk went searching for cures.

CHIPMUNK   *[Studying the ground]* Not here . . . not here. *[He bumps into Elm.]*

CHIPMUNK   *[Looking up]* Wow! Is that you, Elm? You're looking much bigger and stronger than I remember.

ELM   It's been a good last fifty years.

CHIPMUNK	You touch the heavens and can see forever. Did the Manittos make you so tall so you could watch over all their creatures, big and small?
ELM	That has been my understanding.
CHIPMUNK	Can you see the We-mi-am-iki?
ELM	Yes, but it is not a pretty sight. They have become like . . . fish out of water.
CHIPMUNK	I wish we could do something.
ELM	The We-mi-am-iki are too frail. They must learn to develop a tough outer skin like me. Go ahead—punch me. You'll see.

[Chipmunk does and hurts his hand.]

CHIPMUNK	Ouch!
ELM	Yet this same skin makes a tea as gentle as a bubbling brook.
CHIPMUNK	From your bark? What's it good for?
ELM	It stops Disease in its itsy-bitsy teeny-weeny tracks.
CHIPMUNK	*[Excited]* Could I take some back to the We-mi-am-iki?
ELM	I don't thinks so. I saw how they misused fire and lost respect for their animal brothers and sisters.
CHIPMUNK	But they have since learned responsibility and humility.
ELM	What if they decide to make me into a giant pot of tea?
CHIPMUNK	That's the chance you'll have to take.
ELM	Me? Why?
CHIPMUNK	Because the Manittos commanded you to watch out for all creatures, big and small. Right now, their pain is big and their pride is small.
CHIEF 1	And so, Elm gave Chipmunk bark to help the We-mi-am-iki. Unfortunately, he was in such a hurry to get home, he tripped over the bush, Sassafras.

[Elm gives Chipmunk the bark. Chipmunk turns and runs, trip-

ping over a kneeling Sassafras, who immediately turns over as if his roots are in the air.]

SASSAFRAS   Ouch! That's right, run over me. I'm only a little bush, unimportant to anyone.

[Chipmunk tries to turn Sassafras back over.]

CHIPMUNK   Sorry.

SASSAFRAS   Ow, ow, ow! Careful! Oh, no! You ripped my reputable roots!

CHIPMUNK   I said I was sorry!

SASSAFRAS   Well, "sorry" isn't good enough. Not that I expect any respect around here. I'm just a medium-sized plant, nothing elegant like Elm or dainty like Daisy.

CHIPMUNK   Hey! There's nothing wrong with being medium-sized.

SASSAFRAS   You only say that because chipmunks don't run over you every time they're not watching where they're going.

CHIPMUNK   Say, what are "reputable" roots?

SASSAFRAS   The best!

CHIPMUNK   Do you brew them into a tea?

SASSAFRAS   Only if you want to get rid of Disease.

CHIPMUNK   The same as Elm bark?

SASSAFRAS   Different teas for different diseases.

CHIPMUNK   Listen, Sassafras, why don't you come with me back to Ke-ki-on-ga?

SASSAFRAS   Why? So the We-mi-am-iki will have a fixed supply of fancy firewood? So they can scrape their muddy moccasins on my broken branches?

CHIPMUNK   No. They'll treat you with respect. If you provide them with tea, they will tend your every need.

SASSAFRAS   Are you trying to make me a single sullen serviceable slave?

CHIPMUNK   More like a . . . fortuitously fortunate friend.

SASSAFRAS	Wow! Then you'd better plant me near the Meda priest's wigwam. I deserve the best.
CHIEF 1	And so, Chipmunk returned with two strong medicines that made the people well. With good health, pride returned, not the false kind that swells into arrogance, but a joyous kind that mixes with responsibility and humility to make the We-mi-am-iki one of the Great Spirit's noble creations.

[As the chiefs return to their seats, a messenger comes and takes Uncle outside.]

A-SON-DA-KI	[Sarcastically] And what is your message, ———(1) That we should serve the whites like Sassafras?
STONE EATER	Or that we should live in peace until a kind "friend" comes to our rescue?
CHIEF 2	That is not the lesson and you know it. It is: Make the most of your surroundings.
CHIEF 3	Make good use of what you have rather than brood about what you don't. The whites could become that outside friend.
CATFISH	Ah! I am tired of all these children's stories.
CHIEF 4	And I of all your misinterpretations.

[The chiefs begin to argue when Uncle reenters. They stop to listen. The tone of the following debate is less tolerant.]

UNCLE	Tecumseh and Little Turtle have been delayed. Since many of you must leave in the morning, I propose . . .
A-SON-DA-KI	I can speak for Tecumseh. We have tolerated the white man's injustice for too long. There is but one choice: War!
CHIEF 1	We have tried that path before and what has it gotten us? Little Turtle says peace.
STONE EATER	Little Turtle has forgotten the bravery of his youth.
CHIEF 4	Who better understands what it takes to defeat the Long Knives than one who has defeated them?
A-SON-DA-KI	Tecumseh's plan is sound. Together the Miami, the Potawatomi, and the Shawnee will teach the Long

Knives their first lesson in humility.

CHIEF 3   We have tried war before.

CATFISH   And won!

CHIEF 2   And lost!

UNCLE   Please noble leaders, our argument must be with the invaders, not ourselves. Since we seem to be equally divided in this decision, I propose each of you . . .

[Points to the eight chiefs] express your belief, one at a time and without interruption. The rest of us will listen, weigh the facts and consequences, and then meet here first thing in the morning to decide: war or peace?

UNCLE   [To the audience] Your decision tomorrow must unite us as one nation, so listen carefully and remember the Spirit Bird's words: "Know your enemy so well you can outthink him. Go swiftly, act fairly, and kill quickly. If you cannot beat him in a fair fight, then find a way to live in peace."

[The clan chiefs have divided into two groups. Uncle motions for one chief to speak at a time. When the chief is done, he exits until only Uncle remains.]

CHIEF 1   There is no shame in peace. Chipmunk, Flea, and Coyote achieved their goals with their minds, not war clubs. Times have changed. We must adapt to the white man's presence.

A-SON-DA-KI   There would be no shame in peace if this peace was with the Shawnee or the Potawotami. An honorable peace is based on mutual respect. The whites will never respect us. Their idea of respect is to turn mighty Elm into firewood.

CHIEF 4   If we think like Coyote, we can create a treaty that will guarantee respect. If we fight and lose, the Long Knives write the treaty. If we fight and lose, who will care for our orphaned children and widows?

CATFISH   The white man has never honored a treaty. Why would he start now? This is our last and best chance to defeat this enemy. He is not expecting it. We can surprise him the way Bear brought Disease.

CHIEF 2   The whites were tricked at Eel River, Ke-ki-on-ga, and Fort Recovery more easily than Snake by Coyote. Did that end the problem? Did they go away forever? No! They returned with more guns, more soldiers, and a determination not to repeat their mistakes. When you kill one, two return. It is not so with the Miami. Each death creates a hole in the village. The whole nation mourns and a family grieves forever. Like Chipmunk who tripped over Sassafras, we must make the best of our fall.

STONE EATER   You speak like the white leader Harrison. He is certain that we are too weak, too divided, too sleepy to fight in winter. Tecumseh will prove Harrison the one who walks in his sleep. Tecumseh has the wit of Coyote and together we will have the strength and speed of Nan-a-bush. Our cause is just, and for that reason, the Manittos must protect us.

CHIEF 3   Maybe Tecumseh wins a battle or two, but he cannot win the war. They are too many and we are too few. That is not cowardice; it is fact. Coyote tricked Mountain Lion but not Sis-nin-i-koo. As the Spirit Bird says: "If you cannot defeat your enemy, make peace."

LOON   When the whites say "peace," they mean "annihilation." I, for one, prefer to live and perhaps die as our ancestors did: proud, happy, and at one with this land.

[Only Uncle remains to speak to the audience.]

UNCLE: Since there is so much truth in each chief's thoughts, I fear we may never agree what is best for the Miami nation. Still, we must try. Go. We will speak again in the morning.

[Uncle starts to leave when Chiefs 9 and 10 stop him.]

CHIEF 9   Uncle, why did you have us tell stories while we

	waited? What was the lesson you would have us learn?
CHIEF 10	If there was one lesson, why did each chief interpret the stories differently?
UNCLE	The stories tonight revealed the strengths and weaknesses of all the Great Spirit's creatures, but only one showed signs of wisdom.
CHIEF 9	Coyote?

[UNCLE *shakes his head no to each guess.*]

CHIEF 10	Flea? Chipmunk? Nan-a-bush?
CHIEFS 9 & 10	[*Together*] The Spirit Bird?
UNCLE	No! The We-mi-am-iki.
CHIEF 9	How can that be, Uncle? Our ancestors abused fire.
CHIEF 10	And their animal brothers and sisters.
CHIEF 9	And they had to be rescued from Disease by Chipmunk.
UNCLE	The We-mi-am-iki committed all the errors you mention and were weak of spirit besides. But they changed. They survived. The We-mi-am-iki were the only animals to learn from their mistakes. That is the truest sign of wisdom.
	[*Leading the others off stage*] Come. There is much to think about tonight. Your decision tomorrow will prove me right or wrong.

[*They exit. Only the fire remains.*]

THE END

One Good Turn

THIS PLAY WAS FIRST PERFORMED at Royerton Elementary School in Muncie, Indiana, in the spring of 1981, and then again at Brook Park Elementary School in Indianapolis in 1986. It was rewritten in 1997 for this publication.

Characters (in order of appearance)

Mother Goose	Pig #2
Wolf	Pig #3
Little Red Riding Hood	Grandma
Little Red's Mother	Dwarf #1
Scout	Dwarf #2
Queen	Dwarf #3
PIG #1	SNOW WHITE

There is only one rule when putting on this play: every actor should be having a great time. All movement should be exaggerated in the same style as old silent movies and Warner Brothers' cartoons.

COSTUMES: The basic costume is simple: colored T-shirt and jeans. Each actor then wears one or two items that typify his or her character. For example, Red should wear a red scarf, Mother an ugly hat and purse, Grandma an old nightie, Pigs a "squiggle" tail and pig ears, Dwarfs pointed caps and ears, Queen a witch's hat and cape, Scout a baseball cap in reverse, Mother Goose an apron, old fashioned white cap and goose doll, and Wolf a long black tail and a "wolf ears" hood. The director and designer are encouraged to add other suggestive but simple details to the costumes.

SETS: There are no actual sets; rather, the actors create the settings through improvisation and sound effects. The stage is empty when the play begins except for a signpost in center stage with four velcro-attached arrow-like signs. The lettering on the signs must be easily readable by the audience, and should be lettered and pointed as follows:

GRANDMA—pointing stage right
PIGS—pointing stage left
DWARFS—pointing upstage
FOREST—pointing to the audience

The lights should go off and on between scenes and the signpost should be removed or returned. In addition, Mother Goose will help establish place each time she inspects the house or characters at the beginning of many scenes. It is also important that the characters have easy access to the audience [forest] in Scene 7. For safety, I recommend that gym mats be placed around the signpost and remain on stage at all times.

Scene 1: Crossroads; sometime not so long ago

Lights come up first on center stage then the whole stage. Mother Goose enters from upstage right [USR] and crosses to signpost. She is carrying the three books: Little Red Riding Hood, Snow White, *and* The Three Pigs. *While she is deciding which house to visit first, she accidentally drops* Little Red Riding Hood.

MOTHER GOOSE *[frazzled]* My, oh, my! So much to keep track of and so little time! Let's see . . . who should I visit first?

[heads toward Grandma's] Poor Grandma shouldn't be left all alone, but . . .

[heads toward Dwarfs'] the dwarfs have turned their house into a pig sty . . . The pigs!

[heads toward Pigs'] If they work any harder, they'll turn all that straw into gold.

[stops] Oops! Wrong story . . . That settles it. I better check the pigs first. That kind of confusion could set back children's literature for years.

[Mother Goose exits stage left. As soon as she disappears, the Wolf enters from upstage left and crosses to signpost. It should be clear from the beginning that he is not mean, just gruff. He reads the signs aloud as if struggling with his reading.]

WOLF   Forest. No thanks—too dark and scary. Dwarfs. They're so messy that wouldn't be any fun. Pigs. I was there just the other day and they weren't in a very welcoming mood. Grandma. Hey, that's an idea! I haven't seen her for weeks, and she really shouldn't be left alone.

[He starts to leave but then spots the dropped book. He picks it up, sniffs it, and then reads the cover.]

——— (Name of local school) Library. "Little Red Riding Hood."

[looks up] Hey, I know her!

[opens book and reads] . . . and went to Grandma's house . . . Hmm. That's where I'm going too.

[flips ahead and reads] . . . and the hunter pulled out his gun and shot the wolf dead.

[drops book and starts to leave] Interesting story. . .

[freezes, then races back, drops to knees, and rereads]. . . and shot the wolf dead!

[closes book with a snap] Now what kind of ending is that? Bang, bang, shoot the wolf and everyone lives happily ever after. Everyone but the wolf! Well, that's not fair and I won't stand for it.

[stands] I'll write my congressman, the school board. I want this book removed from the shelf.

[Suddenly voices off stage frighten the Wolf, who drops the book and hides behind the signpost. A moment later, Little Red Riding Hood and Mother enter from upstage left (USL) arguing. Mother is carrying groceries and Red is close behind.]

RED   But Mother, why can't I go to Grandma's tomorrow instead?

MOTHER   Little Red Riding Hood, you will do as you are told!

RED   But we're having a baseball game today. I'm batting cleanup and the whole team is counting on me.

MOTHER   So is your grandma!

RED   Please!

MOTHER   No!

                [crossing downstage] Perhaps I could make my point clearer with a song.

RED   *[shocked]* A song?

[Red runs to signpost and picks up book.]

MOTHER   There's nothing as reassuring to a child than the sweet melody of a mother's voice. Mi, mi, mi.

RED   But Mother, there's no song in this story.

MOTHER   *[calling offstage]* Music, please.

[SFX — Ornate, corny overture to nineteenth century type music.]

RED   Wait! Stop the music.

[Music stops. Red then shows her mother the book.]

RED   See? You don't sing a song here.

MOTHER   Just because it's not in the book doesn't mean it can't happen. The right song would inspire you to work hard and trust authority figures.

RED   I'm already inspired. I want to play baseball.

MOTHER   *[starting to leave]* Not until you have taken a basket of goodies to your grandma and that's final.

RED   Ah, Mother.

[Red puts the book back where she found it and the two exit upstage right (USR). As soon as they are gone, the Wolf emerges from behind the signpost.]

WOLF   They think *they* have problems.

                [acts out the following] Knock, knock. Hello, Granny. I thought I'd come by for a visit . . . Wait! Don't shoot!

Bang. Bang. The wolf is going . . . going . . . gone.

[lies down] Well, I'm not going to take this lying down. I'll . . . no. I'll . . . no. I'll . . . yes! Mother was right. Just because it's not in the book doesn't mean it can't happen. Doesn't the Wolf have a right to a happy ending too?

[The Wolf rearranges the signs so the "Grandma" arrow now points to the Pigs' house, the "Dwarfs" arrow points to Grandma's house, and the "Pigs" arrow point to the Dwarfs' house. Some will be upside down but that is okay.

As the Wolf finishes, the Scout enters from stage left [SL] with a map in his hands. He is obviously lost.]

SCOUT	Excuse me.
WOLF	Ahhh! Oh, please don't shoot me, Mr. Hunter. I haven't eaten anyone today.
SCOUT	What?
WOLF	This is really just a disguise. I'm not a wolf at all. I'm a . . . cow. Yeah! Moo! Moo!
SCOUT	A cow? What fairy tale has a cow dress up like a wolf?
WOLF	Uh, "Goldilocks and the Three Cows."
SCOUT	Never heard of it.
WOLF	In short, Goldilocks decides to eat steak and we cows have to hide before we get creamed.
SCOUT	Cow, wolf, bear . . . You can go jump over the moon for all I care. I've got to find Snow White.
WOLF	Snow White? You mean you're not the bang-bang-shoot-the-wolf hunter?
SCOUT	I'm a scout.
WOLF	A knight?
SCOUT	A day or night scout. I go where the action is.
WOLF	Oh, the old kiss-the-sleeping-princess bit. I love that story. Well, the last I heard, Snow White was hanging out at the Dwarfs' house.

SCOUT And where . . . ?

[The Wolf points to signpost.]

SCOUT Ah, yes! Thank you, kind . . . cow.

[He mutters to himself as he leaves] I understand now why some kids don't like to drink milk.

[to Wolf] Good day!

WOLF Good riddance!

[As the Scout exits SR, Red enters from USR, carrying her basket of goodies (which she will carry throughout show). She stops at the signpost just as Wolf hides behind it.]

RED I know why Mother makes me go to Grandma's every week. She wants me to meet some handsome hunter because a hunter would make . . .

[mimics] "such a good provider." Well, I don't want to get married. I want to be a baseball player, a great baseball player.

[looks at watch] Maybe if I hurry, I can deliver these goodies and still get to the game on time.

[reads signpost] Hey, a new way to Grandma's? Hope it's a short cut.

[As she exits SL, the Wolf emerges from behind the signpost and follows.]

WOLF Hope it's not.

[As soon as Red and the Wolf are offstage, the Queen enters from USR, walking very much like a nasty witch. She stops, looks both ways and then relaxes.]

QUEEN Oh, am I beat! Everyday it's the same old thing: Get up, eat caviar, change into this witch's disguise, and then hunt all day for the fairest in the land. I'll bet other queens don't have it so hard. I've walked so far all my warts and moles have turned into corns and blisters.

[looks at signpost] Huh! The dwarfs must have moved. I'll bet they had to. They are so lazy their nicknames should be: Sloppy, Muddy, and Blunder.

[*Queen returns to her witch-like walk and exits SR as the lights fade to black.*]

Scene 2: The Three Pigs' House; moments later

The signpost is removed and the pigs enter. When the lights come up (first on SL, then the full stage), the audience sees the three pigs frozen in a picture-book stance of busy, hardworking pigs. Mother Goose enters from SR, studies them for a moment, checks with her The Three Little Pigs, *and then relaxes.*

MOTHER GOOSE   Oh, how silly it was for me to worry. These pigs are busy little beavers, uh, pigs, working hard on their stick house. Still, they could have saved a lot of time and money in the long run buying brick, but then who ever listens to their Mother . . . Goose. I better go check Grandma.

[*Mother Goose leaves USL and the pigs come to life.*]

[*SFX — construction noises, i.e., jack hammer, regular hammer etc.*]

[*The pigs work diligently until Red enters from SR, stops, and stares in disbelief. The pigs, in turn, also stop and stare. Of course, when they stop, the SFX stop. Suddenly, Pig #1 crosses to Red, studies her, and returns to the others.*]

PIG #1   It *looks* like a little girl.

[*Pig #2 crosses just like Pig #1, except he/she touches her before returning to the others.*]

PIG #2   It *feels* like a little girl.

[*Pig #3 does the same, except he sniffs Red.*]

PIG #3   It *smells* like a little girl.

[*The three then move slowly, sneakily, until they are right beside Red.*]

ALL PIGS   It's the Wolf!

[*They all turn in terror to run, freeze a moment, and then take off one at a time. Each enters and slams the invisible door in the face of the pursuing brother/sister. The three cower behind invisible door.]*

[SFX — slamming door—three times]

[Red now crosses to invisible door and knocks.]

[SFX — knock on door]

RED	Is anybody home?
ALL PIGS	No!
RED	Grandma, are you there?
PIG #1	She left.
PIG #2	Took a vacation.
PIG #3	Left no forwarding address.
RED	But, Grandma, what a strange voice you have.
PIG #1	*[mimicking]* "But, Grandma, what a big mouth you have."
	[as self] You can't fool us, Mr. Wolf. We're wise to your tricks.
RED	Wolf? I'm no wolf!
PIG #3	If you're not the wolf, why aren't you dressed like one.
OTHER PIGS	Yeah!
RED	*[losing patience]* But I'm not the Wolf. I'm a little girl, Little Red Riding Hood.
PIG #2	You're the Wolf in little girl's clothing.
RED	If I was the Wolf, I'd be in sheep's clothing.

[Pig #2 reaches through the door and touches Red's scarf.]

PIG #2	*[to other pigs]* She's right. It's one hundred percent cotton.

[The Pigs huddle in conference for a moment. The audience can hear them mumbling. The following may have to be rewritten so that it fits current sports news.]

PIG #1	All right, if you're really Little Red Riding Hood, who's the greatest Cincinnati baseball player?
RED	*[confused]* Pete Rose.

PIG #3   She's a little Red, all right.

[The pigs open the door.]

RED   Excuse me, but have you seen my grandma?

[The lights face to black.]

Scene 3: Grandma's house; moments later

A cot is set in the SR area. When the lights come up [first on SR, then the whole stage], Grandma is in a picture-book pose of making the bed. Mother Goose enters from USL in a hurry, stops at the invisible door, and opens it.

[SFX — squeaky door]

MOTHER GOOSE Hmm! Grandma really should put a bolt on this door before some nut comes barging in and ruins our story.

[looks around] Well, everything seems all right. I'll just check.

[Suddenly realizes the book is missing] Oh, dear. Oh, my. Oh, horrible! What's happened to the book? I had it in my arms just a minute ago . . . If it should fall into the wrong hands . . . It can't, it won't, it better not!

[Mother Goose runs around in a circle and then begins to retrace her steps. As soon as Mother Goose leaves (SL), Grandma comes to life. She finishes the bed and then crosses to invisible door.]

GRANDMA   For a baseball player, that Red is the slowest person in the world . . .

[notices open door] Hey, who left this door open?

[exaggerates] Being all alone, I hope this does not bode a perilous future . . . Red, are you here?

[SFX — cuckoo clock]

[Grandma makes exaggerated hand-to-ear gesture that she has heard the clock and then yawns.]

Well, I can't wait any longer. It's time for my nap.

[Grandma goes in, lies down and immediately falls asleep. A mo-

ment later, the Scout enters from SL, still lost and confused.]

SCOUT   This must be the place.

[notices open door] Hey, somebody left the door open. I hope this doesn't bode a perilous future for the able Snow White.

[as a hero] Never fear, Snow White. I'm here to help you.

[He walks inside, looks around, and spots the sleeping Grandma.]

Snow White? . . . I'm too late. The Queen has cast a spell on her and turned her into . . . into . . .

[looks closely] . . . a grandma!

[cries and then gets an idea] Of course, that's better than a frog . . . Maybe if I kiss her, I can break the spell and turn her back into a gifted maiden.

[He puckers up and moves in slowly. He is just about to kiss her when Grandma wakes up and screams.]

GRANDMA   Help! Hey, you're not the Wolf.

SCOUT   Don't talk. Just kiss me.

GRANDMA   Wolf! Wolf!

[Grandma jumps out of bed and tries to get away. The Scout remains on his knees beside the bed.]

SCOUT   One kiss and I promise everything will get better.

GRANDMA   I'm not falling for that old line.

SCOUT   I mean it. A single kiss will make you young and talented again.

[SFX — cuckoo clock]

GRANDMA   *[to clock]* Yes, I think so myself.

[to Scout] Okay, I'll kiss you, but first close your eyes.

[While Scout puckers and closes his eyes, Grandma picks up a baseball bat and sneaks up behind him. Meanwhile, the Queen enters from SL just as Grandma hits Scout on the head.]

[SFX — bat hitting a baseball]

SCOUT   *[staggering]* Wow! That kiss was a knockout.

[Scout passes out on the floor. Grandma sets down bat and gets into a position to lift Scout onto the bed, her back to the door.]

[Queen mimicks knocking on door.]

[SFX — knocking on door]

GRANDMA   Come in, Red. Set the goodies by the door and give me a hand.

[The Queen enters and helps lift Scout. Because they are both stooped over, neither sees the other until the Scout is stretched between them.]

GRANDMA   Hey—you're not Red!

QUEEN   [straining] Yeah, but I soon will be.

GRANDMA   I mean you're not Little Red Riding Hood.

QUEEN   [after dropping other half of Scout] Well, you're not ex-actly the Snow White I had in mind either.

GRANDMA   But who are you and what do you want?

QUEEN   I'm the Queen.

GRANDMA   Well, you look more like the Wolf dressed up as a cow.

QUEEN   It's a disguise so I can find the fairest in the land.

[pulls out long royal questionnaire] Let's see if you qualify. Question One: Do you ever cheat on your cake recipes?

GRANDMA   Only if it's Devil's Food.

QUEEN   Question Two: Is it right for a baseball player to steal second?

[While the Queen is asking these questions from the bed, Grandma is circling around her with the baseball bat.]

[SFX — cuckoo clock]

GRANDMA   Yes. Apparently, they come in flocks.

[Grandma swings the baseball bat.]

[SFX — bat hitting a ball for a home run.]

[The two ladies watch as the invisible ball sails off into the sky.]

QUEEN   Foul . . . play.

[*The Queen falls into Grandma's bed and the lights fade to black.*]

Scene 4: The crossroads, moments later

The signpost is put exactly where it was in Scene 1. The lights come up first on CS and then the whole stage. Mother Goose enters from SR and stops at the signpost. As always, she is in a hurry. The book is there, but she doesn't see it.

MOTHER GOOSE   I must have dropped the book at the Pigs' house. Where else could it be?

[*reads signpost*] Pigs? I don't remember it being over there . . . You don't suppose . . . No, I won't even think such a wicked thought.

[*She exits USL. As soon as she is gone, the Wolf enters from SL.*]

WOLF   So far so good. The Hunter is confused, and as long as I can keep Red away from Grandma, I'll never get shot. In this world that's as close as you get to living happily ever after.

[*He rearranges the signs again. This time "Grandma" points to the Dwarfs' house, "Dwarfs" points towards the Pigs' house, and "Pigs" points towards Grandma's place. He finishes and hides just as Red enters from SL and crosses to signpost.*]

RED   No wonder I missed Grandma's house. Now I'm going to have to run to make it to the ball game on time.

[*Red exits USL. The Wolf comes out, planning to follow her, just as Scout enters from SR, holding his map and his head.*]

SCOUT   [*reading map*] I just can't figure this out.

WOLF   Oh, no. The hunter! This time he'll shoot me for sure. I'll just have to pretend I'm a rock.

[*The Wolf drops to all fours and curls up. The Scout continues to walk forward reading his map, but then trips over the Wolf.*]

SCOUT   Funny place for a. . . [*lifts tail*] . . . hairy rock.

[*spots signpost*] Boy, did I have my signals crossed. The dwarfs live over there . . .

[turns map over] . . . I think.

[Scout stands and exits SL slowly, still trying to read his map. The Wolf starts to get up, but the Queen enters from SR, holding her head. She sits on Wolf.]

QUEEN   Whoever would like to fill my shoes should feel my head.

[Her whine leads to a short pause. Suddenly, Mother pokes her head out from DSR and then crosses DS to audience.]

MOTHER   I am appalled by all the confusion that passes as humor in this story. If the world is a stage, then this stage is a bowl of mixed nuts. What this story needs is a message that will inspire children onward and upward to greatness! And what better way to deliver a message than in song. Music, please: Mi, mi, mi.

[SFX — same corny overture from before]

     After all, who knows more about what is best for children than a mother?

[Meanwhile the Queen has jumped up, grabbed the Little Red *book, and hurried to Mother's side.]*

QUEEN   Stop the music!

[pointing to open book as music stops]

     Look! No song!

MOTHER   But the story needs one.

QUEEN   I'm the Queen and I say no!

MOTHER   *[leaving in a huff]* If this was a democracy, I'd sing.

     [to self] Oh, what is this world coming to? If a *queen* dresses like a *witch*, the children will have no role models!

[As soon as Mother is offstage right (OSR) the Queen returns to the rock/wolf.]

QUEEN   It's tough being the Queen. People obey me because they have to, not because I'm right or wrong; and because of my power, I never know who is a real friend. That's why I've got to find the fairest in the land.

[*She sits and the Wolf groans. The Queen jumps up.*]

QUEEN   Either my echo is more tired than I am or I just heard a suspicious character.

[*Since the Queen's back is to the Wolf, he stands and begins to cross SL when the Scout reappears, still reading his map.*]

SCOUT   It doesn't make sense. It can't be that way.

[*The Wolf becomes a rock again, three or four steps from where he was. The Queen circles behind signpost looking for that "suspicious character" and Scout crosses R in front of Wolf. The Queen and Scout never see each other. As the Queen completes her circle, she begins to speak.*]

QUEEN   Something sneaky is going on around here and I'm going to get to the bottom . . .

[*She sits where the rock was and falls.*] That rock . . . and those arrows have moved since the last time I was here. I may be sore, but I'm not stupid.

[*looking at signpost*] Dwarfs. Since I know they're not that way, they just might be that way.

[*She leaves SL just as Scout returns. It looks like he is going to trip again but turns just in the nick of time.*]

SCOUT   There. I think I've got it. If at first you don't succeed, well, you've got three strikes till you're out.

[*While he is talking, Scout folds the map, steps over the rock, and proceeds towards the Pigs' (but marked Dwarfs') house.*]

SCOUT   [*just before he exits*] I've got to get me one of those hairy rocks for the living room.

[*He is gone and Wolf stands up.*]

WOLF   These happy endings are going to be the death of me yet.

[*Exit Wolf USL. Blackout.*]

Scene 5: The Dwarfs' house

The lights come up on USC to reveal the Three Dwarfs frozen in their picture-book pose. They are leaning against each other rather awkwardly, but obviously asleep. As the lights come up to full, Mother Goose enters from SR. She studies the invisible house behind the Dwarfs and then the Dwarfs themselves. When she gets close to them, she holds her nose.

MOTHER GOOSE Hey, these aren't the pigs.

[checks book] These are the dwarfs standing in front of their dirty house. But if these are the dwarfs, who are the pigs? I mean where are the pigs and their stick home? *[snaps her fingers]* The book! Somebody must have found it and moved the house to the forest. Oh, dear. If I don't find it soon, the forest will become a housing development, and Grandma will be out on the streets.

[As Mother Goose exits USR, the dwarfs come to life.]

[SFX — very loud snoring, in rhythm.]

[A moment later, Red enters from SR, circles in front of the Dwarfs, and taps one on the shoulder.]

RED Excuse me . . .

[The snoring stops. The Dwarfs tumble to the ground.]

RED but have you seen my grandma?

[The three dwarfs stand up and run DSL, DSC, DSR.]

DWARF #1 At long last . . .

DWARF #2 Snow White . . .

DWARF #3 has arrived!

[The three run inside the invisible house and point left, right, and up.]

DWARF #1 The dirty dishes are in the sink.

DWARF #2 The broom's in the closet.

DWARF #3 And the unmade beds are upstairs.

RED So?

[The Dwarfs run over and examine Red closely.]

DWARF #1 But aren't you the little girl so desperate for protection . . .

DWARF #2   that you'll clean our house . . .

DWARF #3   for free?

RED   I'm a baseball player, looking for my grandma. You have me confused with someone else.

DWARF #1   But we've waited two hundred years for this moment!

RED   [holding her nose] I believe it!

[The Dwarfs huddle together, mumble something, and reach a happy decision.]

ALL DWARFS   [in huddle] Yes, yes, yes!

DWARF #1   We've decided . . .

DWARF #2   you can clean our house . . .

DWARF #3   anyway!

RED   I don't want to.

[The Dwarfs are shocked and turn away from Red as they speak.]

DWARF #1   Lazy.

DWARF #2   Sloven.

DWARF #3   A disgrace to the human race.

RED   Clean it yourselves.

ALL DWARFS   [like spoiled children] Dwarfs don't clean house.

RED   [turning to leave] Well, neither does this little girl.

[When the Dwarfs realize she is leaving, they follow.]

DWARF #1   But in the movie, Snow White . . .

DWARF #2   loves to clean the house!

DWARF #3   We can show you the video!

[As they exit SR, the lights fade to black.]

Scene 6: The Pigs' House

The lights come up as they did in Scene 2, revealing the Pigs standing exactly as they were in Scene 2. A moment later, Mother Goose enters from USR.

MOTHER GOOSE Since the book isn't here, and the Pigs aren't Dwarfs, then it stands to reason that Grandma is disguising herself as Snow White. . .

[studies Pigs] I can't believe I just said that . . . Hmm. It looks like the pigs are stuck on the same page as before. Whoever found the book hasn't messed up their story, yet . . . I wonder if the Wolf had anything to do with this mess. Naaah. He's too loony . . . the very reason he might do it. Oh, no!

[Mother Goose exits USR and the Pigs come to life.]

[SFX — same construction noises from before]

PIG #1 Work, work, work. I told you we should have avoided sticks.

PIG #2 But brick was too expensive—five ninety-nine a dozen.

PIG #3 That ain't hay!

[SFX — continue construction noises]

[Enter Queen from SR. She stops and stares just as Red did in Scene 2. The pigs likewise stop working and the SFX stops. One by one they run back and forth to inspect the Queen.]

PIG #1 It looks like a witch.

PIG #2 It *feels* like a witch.

PIG #3 It *smells* like a witch.

[The three then cross slowly until they are beside Queen.]

ALL PIGS It's Grandma!

[They all try to hug and pat "Grandma," but the Queen will have none of it. She runs to the door of their stick house, so they can't hide inside. The Pigs treat her behavior as a game.]

QUEEN I don't know what's going on around here, but I'm tired of it. Now tell me which one of you pork chops is Snow White or . . . I'll blow your house down.

PIG #1 Oh, Grandma, what a big mouth you have!

[The others laugh.]

QUEEN Quit hamming it up, or I'll strip your bacon and sausage your pinkies.

PIG #2   Isn't she cute? Grandma's trying to be mean and
               ugly.

PIG #3   Don't tease her. Remember, she's just loining.

QUEEN   [cutting off the Pigs' laughter] Listen, you swine . . .

PIG #1   Hey, that's not nice talk.

PIG #2   Look at that huff-and-puff.

PIG #3   That mouth . . . those teeth . . .

ALL PIGS   It's the Wolf!

[They all turn to run SR, but in their terror freeze, just long
enough for Scout to enter and say his line.]

SCOUT   Excuse me, but are you the Three Dwarfs . . . in dis-
               guise?

PIG #1   [takes off] Run for your life!

PIG #2   [takes off] Every pig for himself!

PIG #3   [takes off] I told them we should buy brick!

[Scout spots the pursuing Queen, screams, and sprints after Pigs.]

                        BLACKOUT

                   Scene 7: Crossroads

The signpost is returned and the lights come up as in Scene 1.
Mother enters and remains as far DSR as possible.

MOTHER   Excuse me, but as a member in good standing of the
               CMPD—Concerned Mothers for Public Decency—I
               want to apologize for this story's continued illogic
               and chaos. Literature for children should always con-
               tain a timely message, such as: "Profit makes Perfect"
               or "Violence is inappropriate except when adminis-
               tered by adults."

[Enter Mother Goose from SL.]

MOTHER GOOSE What's this?

MOTHER   How is this done? With cute songs, pleasing to a
               mother's ear.

[*While Mother talks, Mother Goose sneaks up and studies Mother much like the way the Pigs studied Red.*]

MOTHER GOOSE It's Mother disguising herself as . . .

[*studies her again*] . . . the School Board. I've got to stop her!

MOTHER A good song soothes the soul and carries a message that will inspire children to perfect mother-approved behavior.

[*While Mother is talking, Mother Goose runs around until she finds the* Little Red *book, which she opens and reads.*]

MOTHER GOOSE Look how the story's been changed. Well, there is only way to stop her. Erase!

[*Mother Goose gets out an eraser and energetically erases from book. This has to be timed so Mother gets out only one note of music before she is stopped.*]

MOTHER Music please. Mi, mi, mi.

[*SFX — same corny overture*]

MOTHER [*singing*] You . . .

[*For the next part of this scene, Mother mouths all the words but nothing comes out. She exaggerates her movements believing that everyone can hear her.*]

MOTHER GOOSE Thank goodness I got here in time.

[*reads book*] Oh, dear. Things have really gotten out of hand . . . If everything is to work out, I can see I'm going to have to do some major behind-the-scenes rewriting.

[*Mother Goose exits SR just as the Wolf enters form USL. Mother, of course, sings merrily and silently away.*]

WOLF [*worried*] Now what? Red will be here any minute with no place left to go but her grandma's. And as soon as she gets there, I'm a dead duck, er, wolf . . . I'm afraid I have no choice. I'll just have to speak to her man-to-man, er, wolf-to-man, er, wolf-to-baseball player. It's my only chance to make her understand.

[*Wolf crosses DSR*] Mother?

[She waves to him and continues her silent song.]

WOLF   I think the strain of this story is getting to us all.

[Suddenly, Red enters from USL with the Dwarfs close behind. As
soon as they are on stage, they cut in front of her. Their backs are
to Wolf.]

DWARF #1   I don't understand. We're the Dwarfs. Working for us
             should be a privilege and a pleasure.

DWARF #2   What if we let you work all day Sunday . . .

DWARF #3   From six in the morning to twelve at night?

[Wolf turns and Red spots him. She stiffens with fright.]

DWARF #2   She liked that. Think of something else.

[As each Dwarf makes a suggestion, Wolf gestures, and Red becomes more and more frightened.]

DWARF #1   You can scrub the floors. . .

DWARF #2   dust the furniture . . .

DWARF #3   and cook us twenty-eight meals a week!

[Red screams and runs downstage into the forest (audience)].

DWARF #2   Too much of a good thing.

WOLF   [ignoring Dwarfs] Wait, Red!

[The Dwarfs turn, spot the Wolf, and freeze into a sculpture of
fright. As each finishes his next line, he/she runs into the forest
the same as Red.]

DWARF #1   The Queen has cast a spell . . .

DWARF #2   on the cow . . .

DWARF #3   and turned her into . . .

ALL DWARFS   the Wolf!

WOLF   [following into forest] Please Red. I just want to talk to
             you for a second.

[The following pattern will be repeated. Pig #1 enters from SL,
circles the signpost and talks to Pig #2 before running into the
audience/forest DSL.]

PIG #1   [to Pig #2] Quick! Into the forest!

PIG #2   [to Pig #3] Quick! Into the forest!

PIG #3   [to Scout] Quick! Into the forest!

SCOUT   [to Queen] Quick! They went thataway!

[Scout points DSR. Queen heads DSR and Scout follows Pigs DSL into audience. The Queen then runs up to the singing Mother.]

QUEEN   Quick! They went . . . nuts!

[The Queen goes DSR into audience. Mother finishes.]

MOTHER   [singing final note] . . . Eeee!

[This loud note causes all the characters to come to stop in their tracks and stare at the stage.]

MOTHER   [bowing] Thank you, thank you, thank you. As you
               have just heard, a good message helps create order
               and order guarantees everyone will live happily ever
               after, especially those on top . . . That's all. I've done
               my motherly best. You may continue with your story.

[Mother exits SR, the characters remember where they are, scream, and the chase begins again. Of course, the blocking must adapt to the seating and aisles. Whatever else happens, Red and Scout must accidentally find each other in one area of the audience while the Pigs and Dwarfs find each other in another area (separated by a row of seats). The Queen and Wolf come close but never catch anyone. To draw full focus, the actors should stand up when they speak their lines.]

RED   Mr. Hunter?

SCOUT   Miss White?

QUEEN   [overhearing] Snow White? At last.

[Red and Scout duck. Dwarfs and Pigs pop up one at a time.]

PIG #1   Hey, aren't you the Dwarfs . . .

PIG #2   who live in that dirty house . . .

PIG #3   down the road from the signpost?

DWARF #1   And aren't you . . .

DWARF #2   the hardworking Pigs . . .

DWARF #3   who live in that cheap stick house?

[They are about to shake hands when the Wolf screams.]

WOLF   Hey, Red!

[The six duck down, pop up, shake hands, say their line in unison, and then duck down again.]

ALL PIGS AND DWARFS   Nice to meet you.

[Red and Scout stand. The Queen moves in close.]

SCOUT   There's been some mistake.

RED   I'm not who you think I am.

QUEEN   [surprising both] Me neither.

[Red and Scout run, eventually arriving on stage, beside the signpost. Meanwhile the Wolf has discovered the Pigs and Dwarfs.]

WOLF   Excuse me, but have you seen Red?

[Again, all Pigs and Dwarfs run. Eventually, only the Queen and the Wolf are not on stage. Red then pulls Scout out of crowd.]

RED   Mr. Hunter, do your thing.

[She hides behind the signpost.]

SCOUT   But I'm not a hunter!

[The Dwarfs circle around Scout, then hide beside Red.]

DWARF #1   As a knight . . .

DWARF #2   it's your duty . . .

DWARF #3   to protect us little people from danger!

SCOUT   But I'm not a knight!

[The Wolf is almost back on stage (SL). The pigs get behind Scout and push him towards Wolf.]

PIG #1   Never fear!

PIG #2   We're right . . .

PIG #3   behind you.

SCOUT   [spotting Wolf] Relax, everyone. It's just a cow.

[The three Pigs run up to Wolf where they look, touch, and sniff.]

PIG #1   If . . .

PIG #2   this is . . .

PIG #3   a cow . . .

[They now run over to Queen who is on SR, where they look, touch and sniff.]

PIG #1   Then we were right!

PIG #2   This is . . .

PIG #3   the Wolf!

SCOUT   *[scared]* The Wolf?

[The three Pigs hide in front of the signpost, their tails sticking up in the air. The Scout covers his eyes with one hand and flails pathetically with the other. Meanwhile the Wolf and the Queen approach but do not see each other in CS.]

QUEEN   *[tapping Scout on shoulder]* Could you tell me anything about the fairest . . .

[The Scout jumps into the middle of the Pigs. The Wolf and Queen see each other for the first time.]

QUEEN   A wolf!

WOLF   A witch!

[They both faint. As soon as Red figures out what has happened, she tries to pull Scout out of the pile.]

SCOUT   No, no. Oh please, don't hurt me.

[Finally Red gets Scout to stand up and turn around.]

RED   You know, you're probably the worst hunter I've ever seen.

SCOUT   But I'm not a hunter. I'm a scout.

RED   Same thing.

SCOUT   Not by a high fly. I'm a baseball scout.

RED   Baseball! I almost forgot. I have a game this afternoon and now I'll be late for sure.

SCOUT   Where? It's my business to watch.

RED   *[trying to get her bearings from the signpost]* Well, it's No, it's . . . oh dear! I used to know.

SCOUT   *[pulling out map]* Let's see. We're on the edge of the forest . . . Well, if you ignore these crazy signs, there's a ballpark right down that trail, not far from Grandma's house.

RED   That's right! Say, you're some scout!

SCOUT   And I'll bet you're some baseball player. Come on.

[They begin to exit SR when Mother suddenly appears from SL.]

MOTHER   Hold it right there, young lady. Did you deliver the basket of goodies to your grandma?

RED   No, I couldn't find her.

MOTHER   Well, there will be no baseball until the goodies are safe in her hands. What kind of message would we be giving the world if you got to live happily ever after without doing your chores?

RED   But Mother, this is the chance of a lifetime.

MOTHER   Don't "But Mother" me

[Enter Grandma from SR, baseball bat in hand.]

MOTHER   Mother?

GRANDMA   [taking basket from Red] Is this for me, Little Red?

RED   Grandma, you've arrived just in the nick of time!

GRANDMA   Well, not every hero is male, young, or rides a white stallion.

               [to Mother] How's that for a message?

MOTHER   Well, not bad, I suppose.

GRANDMA   Not bad? It's great!

MOTHER   But Mother . . .

GRANDMA   Don't "But Mother" me . . . Here's your bat, Red. You better go.

               [to Mother] You come with me. I've got another message for you about attitude.

MOTHER   Oh, Mother.

[Grandma and Mother exit SL. Red and Scout exit SR. As soon as they are gone, the Dwarfs pop up and cross DS, very depressed.]

DWARF #1   There goes the old ball game.

DWARF #2   Another foul tip.

DWARF #3   You know, I don't think she wanted to clean our old stone house.

[On the word "stone," the Pigs jump up and cross DS.]

PIG #1   Did you say "stone"?

PIG #2   s-t-o-n-e, like stronger than brick?

PIG #3   Wolf-proof and breath-resistant?

ALL DWARFS   You betcha!

PIG #1   We'll clean your house . . .

PIG #2   outside and in . . .

PIG #3   for only our room and board.

[The Dwarfs extend their hands one at a time.]

DWARF #1   It's . . .

DWARF #2   a . . .

DWARF #3   deal!

[All six exit USL, while the Dwarfs explain all the advantages of stone over brick or sticks. As they leave, the Wolf wakes up and follows a little behind.]

WOLF   Another happy ending for them. It's not fair.

[On the word "fair" the Queen sits up.]

QUEEN   Fair?

[The Wolf is too preoccupied with his own thoughts to be afraid.]

WOLF   Yeah, fair. I brought them together. I made all their happy endings possible.

QUEEN   You didn't make me happy. You scared me to death.

WOLF   Well, you scared me too. I thought you were going to zap me into a frog.

QUEEN   Why? What would I do with a frog?

WOLF   *[gets an idea]* Hey, could you turn me into a hunter?

QUEEN   But you're already a hunter. You're a wolf.

WOLF   That's right. That means I could still be a hero in the story.

QUEEN   But aren't you still afraid of me, the Witch?

WOLF   *[studies her a moment]* Not since we started talking.

QUEEN   At last, a winner!

WOLF   A whiner? Not me. I'm a Wolf who's a Hunter.

QUEEN   *[pulls out questionnaire]* A winner! Look, it's right there, the last question. . .

           [reads] Are you afraid of me, the Witch?

           [to Wolf] You're not. That's the right answer cause it means you didn't judge me by my outward appearance. You're the fairest in the land and I get to take you home.

WOLF   Home?

QUEEN   The castle.

WOLF   The Castle?

QUEEN   Yes. I'm the Queen in disguise.

WOLF   The Queen?

QUEEN   And you shall be the new king!

WOLF   *[sorting it all out]* The Wolf who is really the Hunter is now the new king.

[In his excitement, the Wolf runs offstage, grabs Mother Goose, and drags her onstage. She has a quill pen in hand and wears her writing glasses. Wolf then pulls the book Little Red Riding Hood *from her other hand and reads the last page.]*

WOLF   *[reading]* And they went back to the castle where they ruled justly without guns . . .

           [to audience] Another message.

           [reading again] . . . ever after.

           [after closing book] It's a happy ending for everyone.

QUEEN   That's right. No more contests. No more corns and blisters.

[The Wolf suddenly seems very adult.]

WOLF   You know it's a shame kids don't read more these days. Take this updated classic: Little Red Riding Hood. I think it's going to be even bigger than the original.

[While he speaks, the Wolf escorts the Queen offstage right while Mother Goose stares fondly at them. They are almost offstage

when Mother enters from SL, crosses down to audience.]

MOTHER   *[as elaborately as possible]* The End.

[All three characters on stage cover their ears and the lights fade to black.]

EPILOGUE

[and Curtain Call]

The signpost is removed and the lights come up to full on the whole stage. Mother Goose enters holding the book over her head. All the others are in mass behind her begging to see the book.

MOTHER GOOSE Hold it, hold it, hold it. Now we can't all read the book at once, so I'll turn the pages and show you the pictures one at a time.

[The others agree that is a good idea and form a half circle in front of her.]

MOTHER GOOSE First, the Pigs . . .

[Mother Goose opens the book above her head. The lights go out a moment while the Pigs hurry downstage and freeze as a storybook picture. As soon as they are ready, the lights come back up.]

MOTHER GOOSE working on the stone house.

[turns page] Next, the dwarfs . . .

[The pattern repeats. Mother Goose holds the book above her head, the lights go out, the dwarfs run downstage and freeze in an awkward sleeping position, and the lights come back up.]

MOTHER GOOSE busy helping out.

[turns page] Here's Mother taking a basket of good-ies . . .

[Same pattern with Mother and Grandma DS. Grandma seems impatient and Mother wears a black scarf (like Red's).]

MOTHER GOOSE to Grandma, so they can go together to the ball game.

[turns page] Here's Red and her new friend . . .

[Same pattern with Red and Scout. Red is swinging her bat while Scout admires and takes notes.]

MOTHER GOOSE . . . getting ready for the big game, while the Queen and her new king . . .

[Same pattern with Wolf and Queen, cheering in their pose.]

MOTHER GOOSE . . . root for the home team.

[to self] This has all worked out so well, I may soon write a sequel.

[She laughs, crosses DS, and freezes.]

[Enter a blond girl [DSL] wearing a suit and carrying a briefcase.]

SNOW WHITE Excuse me, could you direct me to the Dwarfs' house?

ALL CHARACTERS [SL] It's Snow White. . .

ALL CHARACTERS [CS] . . . disguised as . . .

ALL CHARACTERS [SR] . . . the Tax Collector!

[Everyone panics, runs in every direction, and exits in all directions.]

SNOW WHITE I guess I got the wrong story!

BLACKOUT.

The History Lesson

THIS PLAY IS NOT ABOUT THE "UNDERGROUND RAILROAD" as much as it is about the tough decisions we all face at all times in history. I wrote this in response to all those reenactors who long for a simpler, better time—that never was. Each epoch is the most difficult. Each generation (including our own) struggles with the tough moral, ethical questions of its age, and only occasionally does "the right answer" seem clear in retrospect.

If it seems I am making fun of the college professor, well, I am. But I also believe almost everything he/she says. His insights about the past are accurate, just incomplete (or in this case, half the picture). His insights about today are also incomplete. Someday people will look back at our time as "the good ol' days."

This play was first produced at Royerton Elementary School in Muncie, Indiana, in the spring of 1982 by the Royerton Drama Club. I was assisted by Ms. Jan Morris and Ms. Jan Addington. The principal was Mr. Kevin Kyle. Since then, the play has gone through two revisions.

Characters

THE PROFESSOR: He/she has given this kind of lecture for thirty years. As his/her energy and health have waned, his love for the past has grown. Of course, he knows nothing of the Crawfords' struggle with the "runaway slave" question. He clings to his notes the way a child does his blanket. This role would best be played by an adult.

WILLIAM CRAWFORD: head of the 1850s household

MA CRAWFORD: his wife

CHARLIE CRAWFORD: her younger brother

LISA CRAWFORD: the oldest daughter, around ten

SALLY CRAWFORD: five years old. She always carries her doll, Betsy.

HAROLD ATKINS: the Crawfords' neighbor. This may be the toughest role in the play. Harold is not a bad man; he simply makes a bad decision. He has grappled with the "runaway slave" question and weighed the facts on an off-balance scale. If he could see himself from our historical perspective, he would cringe in shame. The challenge of this role is to bring out his qualities instead of his weaknesses.

THE AUDIENCE: plays itself during the Professor's lecture, and it plays the Photographer when the Crawfords come alive.

TWO ESCAPING SLAVE

TWO SLAVE CATCHERS

COSTUMES: The costumes should reflect 1850s dress. Ma, Lisa, and Sally wear long dresses while the men wear loose pullover shirts and baggy pants. Since the slides were made from black and white photographs, the costumes should be black, gray, white, or brown. Any objects—and people—who enter a scene and exit before the photo is again a photo can use other colors, but remember: the black and white is what will make the bloody shirt impressive. The Professor wears a full suit and glasses.

THE SET: In the lower downstage right area is a podium. This is where the Professor will give his lecture. Against the upstage right wall is a white sheet or screen, supposedly for the slides. Downstage of the screen is a 6 x 3 x 3-foot dark box that opens from the top and has handles on the sides. Inside are all props the Crawfords will need. The box will serve as a chair, a log, a table, a wagon, and a coffin. Since the Crawford photographs are on slides, a spot light should be projected onto the Crawfords each time the Professor presents a new slide. When the Crawfords come to life, a full set of lights come up on stage right to make the Crawfords seem more natural. Between slides, the stage right area is dark. While the Professor lectures, the actors turn the box to its side, lift the hinged top, get out the necessary props, and prepare for the next slide.

*It is sometime in the late 1850s, some-
where just north of the Ohio River.*

*[When the curtain goes up, the stage is dark and the actors sit on
the upstage side of box, backs to the audience.*

*The Professor enters from the right and crosses the whole
stage. If there is any applause, he stops and bows. He also leaves
a trail of papers on the floor. When he gets to the podium, he
cleans his glasses and then discovers he has lost half his text. He
panics, retraces his steps, haphazardly picks up the papers, and
returns to the podium. The confusion leaves him unnerved.*

*Meanwhile the Crawfords remove their props from the box
and position themselves for Slide #1.]*

PROFESSOR   *[to self]* We're ready, I think.

    [to audience] Good evening, ladies and gentlemen, and
welcome to our third lecture in the series . . .

    [consults notes and reads] . . . "Interpreting Our Pioneer
Past."

    [returns to lecture] Tonight we will focus our attention
on those simple pre-Civil War years when our nation
was awash in innocence and optimism. War would
dampen such exuberance, but at the time families believed that hard work and duty would be rewarded
first in this life and then the next. To illustrate all this,
I have brought slides made from an 1850s family album.

    [to an imaginary tech man in the booth] Could you turn
on the projector please?

[SFX — projector changing slides]

*[The spot comes up and we see the human "slide." It is a family
portrait. Ma Crawford sits on the end of the box (which faces upstage), her broom in her hand. William stands on one side of the
box, Charlie the other, a duffel bag in his hand. Lisa and Sally sit*

on the floor in front of the others. Sally holds a cornhusk doll.
Everyone sits or stands erect with long serious faces.]

[The Professor grabs a pointer from the podium and approaches
the slide.]

PROFESSOR   I would like to present to you the Crawford family, neighbors of ours some one hundred and forty years ago, but residing in someone's attic until recently brought to my attention. I can't tell you what kind of neighbors they were, but I can say: they lived a life of hard work and simple pleasures.

[points to William] William here was a farmer. These hands reveal the man of the house was really the man of the fields. Twelve to fourteen hours a day.

[points to Ma] The woman's place in the family hierarchy is revealed in what's she's called: Ma. No name, no title, but always there, always counted on. Symbolic of her work ethic and family responsibility is this broom, an extension of herself, as necessary as salt, bread, and water. You can bet she never appreciated anything as silly as this photograph.

[points to Charlie] Behind her stands . . .

[consults notes] . . . . Uncle Charlie. Family resemblance suggests he was Ma's younger brother. The duffel bag indicates he was here for a short visit, perhaps the reason for this photograph, and he made his living as a salesman.

[trying to be funny] Maybe this is the fellow about whom someone told the first traveling salesman joke.

[laughs] Here sit their children, Sally and Lisa. I believe it was one of them who identified the album people in a sprawling confident hand. Do you think they felt deprived because they could not grow up to be sports reporters or corporate executives? I think not. Their satisfaction came from duty well done. Security was not a million dollars but rather a family structure that endured the best and worst of times. I

cannot say what became of them except they grew to adulthood, married, raised children, and died almost one hundred years ago.

[As the Professor returns to the podium, he freezes. The lights come up on stage right, and the characters come to life. At first no one moves.]

LISA	Pa, can we move yet?
WILLIAM	Hush, Lisa, or you'll ruin the picture.
MA	Sally, don't slouch.
SALLY	[sitting up] I want to go play.
MA	When the picture is done, you have chores to do.
SALLY	But Ma . . .
WILLIAM	Stop fidgeting, Sally. The pictureman will say when we can move again.
LISA	It seems like we've been here a century.
WILLIAM	[after a pause] All right, we're done. You can relax.

[The children groan and collapse. Everyone else stretches as if they have indeed not moved for a century. When the adults start to talk, the girls begin to play quietly with the doll.]

UNCLE CHARLIE	Imagine—a picture as clear as a lake reflection. Oh, this is an incredible time we live in!
WILLIAM	Unless you're a painter. They'll soon be out of work.
UNCLE CHARLIE	Not if they learn how to use that gadget . . .

[points towards invisible camera and photographer]

UNCLE CHARLIE	. . . and travel around the country like this fellow here. A painter, like everyone else, must adapt to the times.
MA	Painters will never be out of work, not if these pictures are as clear as you say. Who wants their grandchildren to remember all these wrinkles and warts?

[As Ma is talking, a black silhouette enters upstage and crosses behind the family. A few moments later, two other silhouettes follow in pursuit. The audience can only vaguely see what is going on.]

[SFX — dogs on the hunt]

[Over the course of the next dialogue, the two men catch the first, drag him back across the stage, and disappear.]

LISA   Pa, I think I hear something.

WILLIAM   It's nothing. Mind your own business.

MA   *[trying to ignore what is going on outside]* And don't for-get the color. People will miss the color of a painting.

LISA   *[running to door]* I *do* hear something!

WILLIAM   Don't you go outside, Lisa. We're not done.

LISA   But Pa, shouldn't we . . . ?

MA   *[louder]* A painter can work from a sketch or memory. How's this pictureman going to get a herd of buffalo to stand still as long as we just did.

[SFX — a human wail]

SALLY   Ma, is someone crying?

[Uncle Charlie and William hang their heads.]

MA   Let's try one last time. I may have moved in the last photograph, and it will be a long time before the pictureman passes this way again. Lisa, get over here. Pa, put your hands behind your back.

SALLY   I don't wanna take my picture again.

MA   If you sit real still, I'll do your chores for you. We want to do this right.

WILLIAM   Yes. We mustn't mess up this beautiful family por-trait. Charlie, straighten up.

UNCLE CHARLIE   But we can't just . . . ?

WILLIAM   Hush, everyone. The man here has other appoint-ments.

UNCLE CHARLIE   Oh, this is an incredible time we live in.

WILLIAM   Shh! The pictureman will say when we can move again.

[The characters are back in their original positions, when the slide was first shown. As soon as they freeze, the lights go out,

*the spot comes up, and the Professor comes back to life. He uses a
remote to seemingly turn off the projector. The spot goes out and
the Crawfords prepare for the next slide.]*

PROFESSOR   Don't misunderstand me. I'm not saying life was
easy. There were times of drought and flood. Family
emergencies were as common as dandelions. A broken leg was life threatening. Cholera could wipe out a
family in a week. But these same difficulties forced
neighbors to rely on each other. Community spirit
was as necessary as cow's milk. One man's struggle
was everyone's; no family stood alone.

[The Professor points the remote toward the invisible projector.

[SFX — projector changing slides]

*[The spot comes up to show slide #2. Charlie, William, and
Howard Atkins sitting on the box (which now faces stage right).
Each holds a hoe or other field tool. The women are offstage.]*

PROFESSOR   *[using pointer]* Here we have the men folk resting on a
log, taking a break from their heavy field work. This
daily effort makes our jaunt to the spa or health club
seem a tad pitiful, don't you think? The feminine
hand that identified these people says this is "Harold
Atkins, SC." Perhaps the "SC" stands for "Special
Cousin" or "Secret Confidante." We can assume that
this family friend or relation was here to help with
spring planting or field care. Ah, what would poor
William have given to have had male heirs to share
the load? Uncle Charlie is back, proving that some
men worked several jobs to survive and took their ex-
tended family responsibilities quite seriously.

*[The Professor is back at the podium. As he reaches for the re-
mote, he freezes. The lights again come up on stage right.]*

WILLIAM   *[stretching]* I tell you, each year this digging gets
harder and harder.

HAROLD   Well, it's not going to get any easier just staring at it.

UNCLE CHARLIE If you two would work more and talk less, we could
finish this field by noon.

[The three get up and go to work, hoeing and digging in this invisible field.]

WILLIAM   Look who's talking. I've never met a man with more opinions about everything under the sun than you, Charlie.

HAROLD   Speaking of opinions, William, have you thought about what I said to you before?

WILLIAM   I've thought about it, but I'm not sure I've come to any conclusions.

HAROLD   You can't ride the fence forever.

WILLIAM   I know that, but to tell the truth: I'm uncomfortable with either choice.

HAROLD   The law's the law. You've got to do what it says.

UNCLE CHARLIE   What if the law is wrong?

HAROLD   So, you think, young fellow, that you know right from wrong better than our leaders in Washington?

UNCLE CHARLIE   Sometimes, yes.

HAROLD   And what would happen to this country if everyone had your attitude?

UNCLE CHARLIE   Less injustice!

HAROLD   More chaos! You're encouraging anarchy when you say everyone has a right to break the law each time it's a little inconvenient.

WILLIAM   Charlie's upset, Harold, cause we're dealing here with human lives.

HAROLD   Of course we are. A man's life depends on his property.

UNCLE CHARLIE   What about a man's right to free himself?

HAROLD   There are proper ways to do it. Running away isn't one of them. Besides, you're talking here about a slave, not a regular citizen. I think our forefathers addressed your concern when they decided a slave was worth two-thirds of an owner. When it comes to a man's rights, the slave owner has priority.

[At this time, Lisa and Sally enter upstage. They are playing a game and do not notice the men. William, however, is very much aware of them.]

WILLIAM   That kind of thinking seems to be missing something.

HAROLD   If you justify the taking away of one man's prop-
             erty—whatever the reason, you justify someone else
             finding an excuse to steal yours.

WILLIAM   You have a point, Harold.

UNCLE CHARLIE I don't think so. We're talking about human beings
               here, not dirt.

HAROLD   *[reaching down to pick up invisible dirt]* This dirt is what
             makes our good lives possible. The law says we have
             a right to it and a duty to protect the property of oth-
             ers.

UNCLE CHARLIE I'll help you protect your land, Harold, but I won't
               help you catch runaway slaves.

HAROLD   The person who protects the thief is as guilty as the
             thief. All I'm talking about here is neighbor helping
             neighbor.

WILLIAM   You know I've always tried to be a good neighbor.

HAROLD   Then join us. You can make fair money catching run-
             away slaves, and with your hunting skills, you'd be
             good at it.

[William leans against the log/box as in the beginning of this scene. The others soon join him. The girls leave.]

WILLIAM   I don't know. It doesn't sound right.

HAROLD   Either you're for us or against us. There ain't no in-
             between.

UNCLE CHARLIE Slave catcher: killer of human dreams.

HAROLD   It may be the only way to keep this country together:
             just do what's right for yourself and your southern
             neighbor.

WILLIAM   I'll think about it, Harold.

*[The three freeze. The lights go off; the spot comes on. The Pro-
fessor comes back to life. He picks up the remote and flicks it to*

turn off the projector as before. The spot goes out and the Professor continues.]

PROFESSOR Life was up at five, work till dark, and in bed by eight. Uh-oh—where'd it go?

[hunts through papers, tossing some over his shoulder]

Ah! Here it is! *[reads first sentence]* "Insecurity today has become a way of life." Think about it—free time means more time to doubt. With fewer chores to do, children are bored or get into trouble. Adults suffer heart disease, anxiety attacks, and a sense of isolation. Our ancestors charged through life; we flit and flutter.

[leaves podium] The next slide is of a family meal. Oh, what a difference a hundred and fifty years can make. In those days, a stranger was welcomed the same as a foreign ambassador. Mother would get out the white sugar and the butter molded to look like strawberries. If the children were included, they knew manners are as sacred as a religious ritual.

[The Professor turns the remote to the invisible projector but does not go to slide as yet.]

[SFX — projector changing slides]

[The spot comes up to reveal Slide #3, the Crawfords at the dinner table. Charlie and William are seated: arms crossed and serious. Lisa and Ma stand behind. All heads are bowed slightly. All food and plates are invisible.]

PROFESSOR Today we see each stranger as a potential intruder and we don't talk to neighbors for months as a time. Fast food has replaced the family meal and conversation is limited to what is on TV.

[approaches slide with pointer] Hmmm! You can almost smell the fresh baked bread, the garden vegetables, and the bubbling stew. No problem here with canned taste or chemical preservatives.

[points to men] Notice how the men sit with arms folded and the women serve the food. They would

have been shocked by our notion that everyone eat together at the same time. Why? Because survival depended on cooperation. Each person had a role; success was a team performance, without a sense of competition. In those days, no woman doubted her unique place in the family, while today's women strive to be "just one of the boys."

[The Professor is back at the podium. He freezes, the spot goes out, and the regular SR lighting brings Slide #3 to life.]

WILLIAM   *[praying]* And for these blessings, we thank Thee.

ALL   Amen.

UNCLE CHARLIE   *[picking up invisible spoon]* Yum, yum!

[slurps his invisible soup]

MA   Charlie, eat your soup; don't inhale it. Set an example for the children.

     [addressing invisible photographer] Mr. Pictureman, as soon as you've put away your things, I hope you will join us.

WILLIAM   *[to photographer]* Soup's great. Ma's specialty.

[SFX — knock at door]

SALLY   *[offstage]* I'll get it!

[Sally comes out of nowhere (USR), circles the table, and opens an invisible door (DSR)].

MA   Don't run in the house.

SALLY   Hi, Mr. Atkins. Come on in.

[Harold enters. There is an immediate tension in the room. Of course, Ma understands what is going on. She just pretends not to.]

HAROLD   *[to Sally]* Hello, Sally. How's Baby Betsy?

SALLY   *[holding up doll]* She's been sick, but look. Now she's better.

HAROLD   It's the spring weather—warm one day, freezing the next. Just keep Betsy bundled up each time you take her out.

[Sally exits the same way she came, running around the dining table, stopping to talk to doll, and then exits stage right.]

SALLY   See how she likes to run, Mr. Atkins.

[pauses and scolds doll] But not in the house.

[There is a long tense silence before William speaks.]

WILLIAM   Harold, this is a pleasant surprise. Sit down and join us.

MA   Lisa, go get Mr. Atkins a plate.

[Lisa exits the same as Sally but without the energy.]

HAROLD   I'm sorry, Mrs. Crawford, but I've got work to do.

MA   At this hour?

HAROLD   William, I came by to see if you'd be going hunting with us tonight.

MA   Hunting?

HAROLD   What we talked about before.

UNCLE CHARLIE   He's not interested. He'd got work to do here, and it's too late to go out tonight.

HAROLD   I think William is capable of answering for himself.

WILLIAM   Yes, I think I'm capable.

UNCLE CHARLIE   It's the wrong time of the year, William. You could catch Betsy's cold.

HAROLD   Bundle up.

UNCLE CHARLIE   And what are you going to find? It's spring. You'll only catch fawns and cubs.

HAROLD   Not so. I got word a fat flock is coming from the South tonight. You'll find the air invigorating, the exercise sound, and you'll work with the knowledge you're doing the right thing.

WILLIAM   Maybe I should.

UNCLE CHARLIE   No! Ducks have already gone north. I haven't seen a goose for weeks.

HAROLD   The rewards could make living a lot easier, William. You won't have a harvest again till fall.

UNCLE CHARLIE	You don't want to do that. You're not the kind who preys on the weak and frail.
MA	What are you talking about? Harold, I insist you sit down and eat.
HAROLD	Can't.
MA	You won't try my soup?
WILLIAM	Soup's great. Ma's specialty.
HAROLD	We have our duty, William, our patriotic duty.
WILLIAM	What kind of duty won't let you sit down and join us for a bowl of good soup?

[Lisa enters with bowl.]

MA	Lisa, serve Mr. Atkins some soup.
UNCLE CHARLIE	Yes, Harold, join us. Give those poor creatures a chance to grow up. Quail and turkey are with brood. What joy can there be in shooting fawns and cubs?

[Lisa serves the soup.]

MA	Eat your soup, Harold . . .
HAROLD	You know, William, you risk everything by not going with us. The country's stability depends on north-and-south cooperation. If you work against us, the authorities will confiscate everything you own, including this good soup.

[Harold opens the invisible door and leaves in a huff.]

MA	*[continuing]* . . . before it gets cold.
LISA	Doesn't Mr. Atkins like soup, Pa?
WILLIAM	Maybe he wasn't hungry.
UNCLE CHARLIE	Or he's got a different kind of appetite.
MA	I've never seen a man so upset about doing "the right thing."
UNCLE CHARLIE	That kind of upset turns good men into dangerous enemies.
MA	You two be careful.
WILLIAM	Me? I haven't done anything. Harold knows I'd do

anything for him and his family. Why has it come to this? Why can't it be like it was when helping your neighbor meant working for a common good?

UNCLE CHARLIE Maybe it was never that simple, William. We just thought it was.

[Sally enters holding up doll.]

SALLY Ma, I think Betsy's sick again.

MA [after inspecting doll] She'll be all right. Just keep her inside for a day or two. Now go put her to bed.

[Sally exits. The others take their positions when the photo was first taken.]

UNCLE CHARLIE I've kind of lost my appetite.

WILLIAM [praying] Oh, Lord, give us wisdom now, when we really need it.

ALL Amen.

[They freeze. The lights go out and the spot comes on. The Professor comes back to life and uses the remote to seemingly turn off the projector. The spot goes out. The Crawfords prepare for Slide #4.]

PROFESSOR So how far have we come in a hundred and fifty years? Achievement is measured in dollars and cents; satisfaction on an excitement meter. Too many turn to drugs to get high and count on pills and counseling to get through the lows. No day is complete without an adrenaline rush, while Madison Avenue and Hollywood continue to set the standards of human worth.

[He uses the remote to turn on Slide #4 (SFX—projector changing slides), but does not approach it yet. The box is now a wagon (at a downstage angle) with William and Lisa standing beside it, fishing poles in hand.]

PROFESSOR Back in the 1850s, simple pleasures fulfilled simpler expectations. If you needed an adventure, you went on a bear hunt. Beauty had four unique seasons, climaxing with a spring "sugar snow" or the rainbows of fall harvest.

[leaves podium] If the world seemed larger; it also seemed grander. The Middle East was a fairy tale and Europe's problems too far away to be real. California gold had put a sparkle into everyone's imagination, and each region—north, south, east, and west— knew it was God's favorite. "Unemployment" was another word for laziness, "inflation" what you did to a balloon, and "pollution" was no more threatening to human survival than a pair of dirty socks.

[crosses to slide with pointer] Here we have a father and daughter preparing the horse and wagon for a fishing trip. Who has time for it today? Who knows a good fishing hole that doesn't cost a fortune to get to? I'm saying . . . I'm saying, for the same reason a day's work couldn't be measured by a clock, fulfillment came from finding more in less. Harmony was a communal knowledge that linked place and responsibility. Right and wrong came in fewer shades of gray.

[The Professor returns to the podium where he freezes. Again the lights come up SR and the spot goes out.]

WILLIAM *[coming to life]* Thanks again, Mr. Pictureman. Come on, Lisa. Climb up there so we can go catch us some little tiny fish.

[Lisa and William sit on the box as if on the front of a wagon. He picks up some invisible reins and the two jiggle slightly as they drive along.]

LISA Pa, why did you say "little fish"? Don't we want the big ones?

WILLIAM No, Lisa. Safety comes first. I won't let you keep anything bigger than four foot.

LISA Four foot? That's huge!

WILLIAM Not in the old days. When I was young, fishing was considered more dangerous than shooting. Until I

	was twelve, I wasn't allowed to bait the hook for fear of attracting the big ones. I lost two of my best friends when instead of bringing home lunch, they became some fish's dinner.
LISA	*[suspicious]* What were their names?
WILLIAM	"Has" and "Ben."
LISA	Never heard of 'em.
WILLIAM	When it came time to divide up the chores, I used to beg your grandpa: "Make me clean the barn, make me shingle the roof, but please don't make me go fishing." On the poor fishing days, I'd get home and have to stay in bed a week.
LISA	Were you wore out?
WILLIAM	Punishment.
LISA	For not bringing home enough fish?
WILLIAM	For bringing home too many.
LISA	But you said it was a "poor fishing day."
WILLIAM	You forget: fish travel in schools. Well, I'd catch one, and all the rest would follow. And if you tried to run away, they'd track you. One day, when I wasn't paying proper attention, three trapped me. Two held me down while the other tickled my tummy.
LISA	That's funny.
WILLIAM	For you maybe, but not for me. When I got home, I stunk so bad no one would speak to me for a week. The worst time came during a drought. As the river shrank, the fish got braver, stalking our farm for food and water. That summer, no child was allowed out after dark.
LISA	Because the fish would eat them?
WILLIAM	Well, we didn't want to find out. Why, to save the farm animals we had to put the barn up in a tree.
LISA	You can't put a barn up a tree!
WILLIAM	That was the easy part. The hard part was milking the cows: If it was windy the night before, it would

shake the barn so much that all you'd get was butter.

LISA   Those fish sound pretty smart.

WILLIAM   Not that smart. They never could figure out how to shinny up that tree. Many a morning we'd come out and find fresh fin marks all around the base, and down by the river you could hear them all coughing from having scratched their chests on the bark. That tree barn saved the cows, but it put those fish in a *fowl* mood.

LISA   A *foul* mood?

WILLIAM   They started eating our chickens.

[SFX — someone running]

LISA   What's that?

[William pulls the reins to stop the invisible horse. Lisa stands. William peers to his right.]

LISA   Someone's coming.

WILLIAM   Get down.

LISA   He's being chased.

WILLIAM   Get down.

LISA   We've got to do something.

WILLIAM   [pulling her] I said, get down.

[William pulls Lisa down and covers her to protect them both.]

[This next section is a slide show. The SR lights go out. The spot with the accompanying SFX of the projector changing slides. In a series of five or six pictures, the audience sees the slave running and the pursuers after (Harold Atkins is one). Eventually they catch the slave, beat him, and drag him away. The last slide has the slave turning towards the wagon.]

RUNAWAY SLAVE [whispering] Help me.

[The slave drops a garment and the lights go to black. A moment later, time enough for Slave and Slave Catchers to exit SR, the regular lights come up on SR. William and Lisa sit up.]

LISA   Pa, why didn't we do something?

WILLIAM   There was nothing we could do.

LISA   Maybe we could've hid him.

[The two climb down from the wagon and move to the garment.]

WILLIAM   If we had interfered, we would have gone to jail.

LISA   Pa, it wasn't right!

WILLIAM   They would have taken our house, our land—every-thing we hold dear.

LISA   [pointing to the dropped garment] Oh, Pa, look! They beat him bad!

[William picks up the bloody garment (the audience must see the red!) and carries it back to the wagon. There he tosses it in back out of sight. Lisa gets down her fishing pole and stands as she did when Slide #4 was first shown.]

WILLIAM   [to self] Is this the price we pay to save our country? Are property rights the excuse for this?

LISA   Let's go home. I don't want to go fishing no more.

WILLIAM   [getting pole and standing as in Slide #4] Barns in trees with fish on the prowl contains more truth than the lies we sometimes tell ourselves.

[The lights go out. The spot comes up, and the Professor comes back to life. He reaches for the remote and again turns off the imaginary projector [spot]. The Crawfords prepare for the next slide and the Professor continues his lecture.]

PROFESSOR   History is an old picket fence whitewashed so often we sometimes forget the pattern of the original grain. These photographs give us a chance to peel away the paint, so to speak, to see the past the way it really was. Back then, most family pictures were portraits. Everyday life was considered unworthy of photo-graphic immortality. That's why I feel so fortunate to have this next slide.

[The Professor points the remote towards the invisible slide pro-jector. The spot comes on for slide #5.]

[SFX — slide projector]

[Slide #5 is of the three women doing domestic work. Ma cooks over an invisible fire, Lisa churns, and Sally sets the table. All three have stopped what they are doing to stare at the camera. Sally holds her doll, Betsy. As the slide comes up, the Professor accidentally knocks his glasses off with the remote. They sail onto the floor. He has to get onto his knees to find them.]

PROFESSOR   Oh, dear! I can't see. How am I supposed to explain what's going on if I can't see myself?

[finds glasses but stays on floor] This is what I was trying to tell you. We now have microwave ovens, computers, projectors, and contact lenses in a variety of cheerful colors. They are supposed to make us free; but instead, we can no longer live without them. We're grown dependent on this so-called progress. Technology has made slaves of us all.

[The Professor stands and returns to slide with pointer.]

PROFESSOR   Here we have the three ladies of the Crawford family busy doing domestic labor. Notice how the daughters dress the same as their mother, symbolic of their respect for the parent. No strife between generations here. Mother cooks, older daughter churns, and even the baby contributes by setting the table. Dinner here is a half day occupation. We have no respect for such effort today. Our freedom to eat junk foods means we have sacrificed palate for multiple careers. Lunch for us is a chore; for the Crawfords, an event. You might say, we have our cake and eat it too. We just can't taste it.

[The Professor returns to the podium and freezes. The spot goes out and the main SR lights come up. The women come to life.]

MA   Mr. Pictureman, you wasted your time with that one. No one will ever want to see us all so . . . humdrum. Please stay for supper. Mr. Crawford will be back any minute.

SALLY   Should I put out a fork and spoon for Uncle Charlie?

MA   I don't know if he'll be back tonight.

SALLY	I will. Then he'll have to come back.
LISA	Uncle Charlie's been gone a long time.
MA	And he might be gone a lot longer.
LISA	You say that like you're mad.
MA	I worry.

[Sally finishes her chore and sits down to play with the doll.]

LISA	You wish he didn't work for the Underground Railroad, don't you?
MA	I wish there was no need for it.

[SFX — knock on door]

SALLY	Uncle Charlie!
MA	Your uncle wouldn't knock. Whoever it is, not another word about Uncle Charlie! Do you understand?

[Ma's plea is also made to the photographer. Both girls nod. Lisa crosses down to invisible door and opens it.]

LISA	[formal] Mr. Atkins . . . Please come in.
SALLY	[energetic] Mr. Atkins! Mr. Atkins! [She holds up the doll.]
HAROLD	Hello Sally. Hello Betsy. You're both looking well. Mrs. Crawford, I came by to speak with William.
MA	He had errands up north, but we're expecting him for supper.
HAROLD	[suspicious] He seems to be doing a lot of traveling lately.
MA	[nervous] Yes. Rumor has it they'll pay more up there for grain this fall.
HAROLD	Odd! The Ohio River's been the best place to sell your grain for years. Well, tell him I stopped by, will you? Your dinner smells delicious.
SALLY	Aren't you going to stay, Mr. Atkins?
HAROLD	I'd love to, Sally, but I have work to do. Tell me, where's your Uncle Charlie?
SALLY	I'm not supposed to say.

HAROLD	[getting close to Sally] Well then, don't tell me yourself. Have Betsy do it: Betsy, where's Uncle Charlie?
SALLY	[in a high voice while holding up the doll] He got a job on a train.
HAROLD	Where?
SALLY	[turning to Ma for help] Where'd you say?
HAROLD	Kentucky?
SALLY	Yes, he's working for a train in Kentucky.

[Of course, the others are dying with anxiety, but there is nothing they can do.]

HAROLD	Oh, that's a dangerous place what with all those criminals helping slaves to escape. But don't worry, Sally, I'll have my friends keep an eye out for him. [to Ma] I think the fall's the best time of year for hunting, don't you, Mrs. Crawford. You find tracks . . . almost everywhere. Much obliged for the warmth and hospitality.

[He leaves through invisible door.]

LISA	Sally, you weren't supposed to tell!
MA	Lisa, leave your sister alone.
LISA	But now Mr. Atkins knows all about Uncle Charlie!
MA	He already knew, and your Uncle Charlie knows to be careful.
LISA	But Mr. Atkins will tell his friends and they'll all be after Uncle Charlie.
MA	Hush, Lisa. It does no good to worry. And when he comes home, you mustn't show you've worried.

[Lisa starts to churn the butter, but she is still upset. Ma notices.]

SALLY	Ma, did Betsy say something wrong?
MA	No, child. How can it be wrong to tell the truth? Betsy's been acting so grown up, soon she'll have her own chores to do. [to Lisa] Lisa, when you finish the butter, I want you

to make some blueberry muffins, your uncle's favorite. That way if he does show up, he'll know we were
thinking about him.

[Lisa does not respond. She has frozen in the position of Slide #5.
So does Ma.]

SALLY   It'll be a surprise. When Uncle Charlie comes, we'll
get out the muffins and say "surprise."

[to Betsy, scolding] A surprise is a secret. You mustn't
tell anyone!

[Sally returns to rearrange a fork (as she was for Slide #5) and
everyone freezes. The lights go out, the spot comes up, and the
Professor comes back to life. He immediately picks up and points
the remote in the direction of the invisible projector. The spot goes
out.]

PROFESSOR   What is life worth today? What was it worth back
then? Medicine has given us twenty more years of
life. but what do we do with it? Gang killings, "road
rage," and pin-point missiles have cheapened indi-
vidual life. We'd be shocked if the local newspaper
didn't include an article about world hunger, mass
murder, and child abuse.

[leaves podium] Today we race through life pretending
death doesn't exist. We grieve for an afternoon and
then it's back to work. For the Crawfords, mourning
lasted a year, and people died in their own beds with
family close and everyone confident of the
deceased's eternal reward.

[The Professor uses the remote to turn on projector. The spot
comes up on Slide #6. The box is now a coffin and the family
stands beside it on both sides. The characters should be wearing
something that is symbolically black but which can be removed.
During the time the SR area was dark and the top of box up, the
Escaped Slave enters in a way that the audience does not see.]

[SFX — slide projector]

[The Professor returns to podium to pick up pointer before going
to slide.]

PROFESSOR   Our last slide comes with no ornate feminine hand to explain who has died of what. Since no cleric leads the way, we can assume the passing was quick and unexpected. Notice how the coffin is unadorned, a vehicle of transition not of permanent stay. Ma's expression indicates it is Uncle Charlie. He is the only family member not present. My concern, however, is not who died as much as what was said. Oh, how I would love to return to this peaceful time and hear the words of praise and feel again the comfort of their message.

[This time the Professor freezes while looking at the picture. The spot goes out, the SR lights come up, and the Crawfords again come to life.]

WILLIAM   Thanks again, Mr. Pictureman. I'm beginning to think of you as one of the family.

[to family] You all know what you have to do. Sally, you're not to say a word, understand?

LISA   Here he comes.

[Sally nods. William begins a prayer.]

WILLIAM   Lord, we only ask that we be instruments of Thy will . . .

[as if he's been talking awhile] . . . and that's why we admired Charlie so. No one will doubt he was a giving man, always put others in place of himself.

[During this prayer, Harold and two other slave catchers enter.]

HAROLD   I'm sorry, Mrs. Crawford. I didn't know.

MA   You might as well have shot him yourself.

HAROLD   I assure you I knew nothing. Neither I nor my men had anything to do with it.

[Mrs. Crawford turns her back.]

HAROLD   William, normally I wouldn't disturb you . . .

WILLIAM   Say your piece, Harold.

HAROLD   My friends here believe they saw a runaway slave cross onto your property last night.

WILLIAM	They didn't.
HAROLD	I'd like to have your permission to check. I don't need it, but I'd feel better to have it.
WILLIAM	There are no runaways on my land, Harold. Take my word for it.
HAROLD	I need to check.
WILLIAM	No.
HAROLD	It would do a lot to eliminate suspicion that you and Charlie—may he rest in peace—have been harboring slaves.
WILLIAM	If I let you search my place, Harold, promise it'll be the last time.
HAROLD	I hope it will be.
WILLIAM	Help us load the coffin onto the wagon, and I'll take you around the place myself.

[The four men lift the coffin, carry it in a circle and then pretend
to load it onto a wagon. The coffin then becomes the wagon.
Sally, Lisa, and Ma climb on. Ma holds invisible reins.]

WILLIAM	You take the wagon north, Ma. I'll catch up just as soon as Harold finishes his search.
HAROLD	North? It's none of my business, but why north?
MA	You're right. It's none of your business.
WILLIAM	Much of Ma's family is from up north.
SALLY	We're going to see Uncle Charlie up north.
MA	[after a moment of fear] That's right, Sally—we're going to see that Uncle Charlie gets there.
WILLIAM	[to Ma] Take your time. I'll be there as quick as I can. [to Harold and others] Now where did you see that slave? And what makes you so sure he stayed on my property?

[They all exit stage left.]

LISA	There'll be a frost tonight, Ma. How far do we have to go?
MA	The next station's about twenty miles.

[*The twenty mile journey is another slide show. The SR lights go out, the spot comes up, the characters freeze. Five times, the spot goes out, the characters change positions and freeze and spot comes back up. Finally, the spot goes out, the regular SR lights come up, and the characters move like normal, jiggling slightly because of riding in the wagons.*]

SALLY   Me and Betsy are cold.

MA   I think this is the place. Whoa!

[*Ma brings the wagon to a halt. Everyone gets off and Ma opens the coffin. The Escaped Slave climbs out.*]

ESCAPED SLAVE Oh, my back!

MA   I'm sorry. I didn't dare let you out sooner for fear of someone riding by.

[*Uncle Charlie emerges, duffel bag in hand, and gives everyone a hug.*]

UNCLE CHARLIE You sure took long enough to get here!

LISA   We had to bury you first.

UNCLE CHARLIE What?

MA   The young man here was spotted. We had to fool Harold and his gang.

ESCAPED SLAVE It's so cold here, and it'll be worse in Canada. How will I get word to my family?

UNCLE CHARLIE There's a fire with food over there. We'll talk about getting word to your family later.

[*The Escaped Slave leaves.*]

MA   [*privately*] You can't come home no more, Charlie. If Harold saw you, he'd know what we've done.

[*William enters.*]

MA   How'd it go, William?

WILLIAM   Harold found where we fed the poor man. I had to make up a lie I wouldn't believe myself.

UNCLE CHARLIE Do you think he'll follow?

WILLIAM   No, but we mustn't take any chances. Charlie, I'm afraid you can't ever . . .

UNCLE CHARLIE   I know.

LISA   What? Uncle Charlie's not coming back with us?

WILLIAM   Not for a while.

MA   I don't trust that Harold Akins. If he figures we fooled him, he'll find a way to get even.

WILLIAM   It's the lying all the time that bothers me most. Even when it's necessary, it's still a lie.

[The group takes off any mourning clothing and gradually resets itself as in Slide #1.]

SALLY   Uh-oh. Betsy's sick again.

[SFX — movement in the bushes]

MA   What was that?

WILLIAM   Hush! Be still!

MA   It's probably just an animal.

WILLIAM   Nobody move!

UNCLE CHARLIE   Are you sure Harold didn't follow?

WILLIAM   Quiet!

LISA   *[after a pause]* Pa, can we move yet?

MA   Shh!

LISA   It seems like we've been sitting here a century.

UNCLE CHARLIE   Oh, this is an incredible time we live in.

WILLIAM   Hush now. The pictureman will say when we can move again.

[They freeze. The SR lights go out and the spot comes on. The Professor comes back to life.]

PROFESSOR   Oh, dear! I seem to have been daydreaming. Now where was I?

   [looks at slide] Oh, yes. We're done. Back to where we started . . . In conclusion . . .

[He returns to podium where he turns off the projector with the remote and then rifles through his notes.]

PROFESSOR   My conclusion is I've lost my conclusions. I'll just say this: I wish we could learn from the past. If only we could slow down, turn off the TV, and return again to that simple time when a field of blueberries was a double high: fun to pick and fun to eat later in muffin or pie. Maybe someday, but not today.

[looks through notes] Next week our lecture will be . . . will be . . . will be . . . ah . . . "Songs of the Civil War." Beauty out of chaos. I swear, some of you will want to put on a uniform and run off to war. Well, until then, thank you for coming and good night.

[The Professor starts to leave in the wrong direction, has to go back for his notes, continues in the wrong direction, corrects himself and leaves.

Lights fade to black.

The curtain call should be done as a series of slides with spot and SFX of the slide projector. Escaped Slave, Slave Catchers, Harold, Lisa and Sally, Uncle Charlie, William and Ma, and the Professor. The last slide should be of the whole group working together.]

THE END

Doll Sense

based on the book THE MEXICAN DOLLHOUSE
by Lucina Ball Moxley

THIS IS A PLAY ABOUT INTOLERANCE AND MISUNDERSTANDING. Although it focuses on three ten to twelve-year-old girls, it is really about all of us trying to get along. Adults live in a world apart, and the children only have a vague idea of what goes on in the dollhouse.

For those loyal readers of Mrs. Moxley's books, I apologize for having cut so many favorite characters and scenes. There is only so much space on a school stage and so much money in the school coffers. My goal is to make the play entertaining (for boys as well as girls), accessible, and affordable.

SETTING: The stage area is divided into two parts. The far right will usually serve as the living room/dining room of the dollhouse. The audience sees a sofa, side table with lamp and phone, a cupboard, a dining table with two chairs, and a TV. When the TV is on, the audience can see light. They never see the picture or hear the sound.

The stage left area is Nancy's bedroom, but the only furniture the audience sees is the table with the Dandy dollhouse. The dollhouse should be large enough to hold real dolls and have a downstage chimney. It looks a bit ragged and the roof comes off. When the girls move their dolls inside the house, the audience should see the movement in the stage right area. Remember to dress the real dolls the same as the character dolls.

At the beginning of the play, the dollhouse is in place as part of Nancy's bedroom. Later on, this area will become the school yard (signified by a bench) and—at another time—the front yard of Katie's house (signified by a small bush and door in the background.)

Ideally, the lights on the two areas would operate independently. Since most schools will not have such facilities, one set of lights that turn off and on will suffice.

COSTUMES: Since I have updated the play to the present, most of the costumes can come from the actors' own wardrobes. The adult dolls should wear token adult wear. For example, Jim Dandy might wear a suit and dress hat and Grandma Dandy a shawl. I recommend that Rosalinda wear regular clothes and her dolls wear only token Mexican apparel. For some in the audience, traditional costuming will come across as stereotyping. (It's an interesting dilemma: we want people to be proud of their heritage and at the same time we want to avoid labeling.)

SOUND: Marie's voice should be recorded: deep, slow, artificial to the audience but normal to the girls. Each time the girls come to the bedroom, the audience should hear footsteps coming up the stairs. There will also be the sound effects (SFX) of a boy groaning twice and a grandmother groaning once, a school bell, running children, a car passing by, and the heavy boom of a giant walking.

Characters

People:
NANCY: the ten- to twelve-year-old owner of the dollhouse. She wears a leg brace.
KATIE: Nancy's best friend for years
ROSALINDA: the new girl in the neighborhood, originally from Mexico
MARIE JOHNSON: Nancy's mother. The audience never sees her. She is just a voice from offstage.

Nancy's Dolls:
GRANDMA DANDY: wisest of all the dolls
JIM DANDY: Father of Tommy, son of Grandma Dandy
TOMMY DANDY: a ten- to twelve-year-old boy doll
SANTA CLAUS

Katie's Dolls:
MAMA JEAN DEAR: Bobby's mother
BABY SARAH DEAR: a doll always in Mama Jean's arms
BOBBY DEAR: a ten- to twelve-year-old

Rosalinda's Dolls:
  HORACIO VALDEZ: the father
  SUSANA VALDEZ: the mother
  LOLITA VALDEZ: the ten- to twelve-year-old daughter

Scene 1: inside the dollhouse, the present

When the audience is being seated, the doll furniture is in place but no one is on stage. When it is time to begin, the lights fade to black and the dolls enter. Grandma Dandy is sewing on the sofa. Jean Dear and Jim Dandy are looking over some house drawings on the kitchen table. Tommy and Bobby sit downstage on the floor playing chess. Because there are no humans present, the dolls are moving and acting like humans.

TOMMY	*[after moving a piece]* Checkmate.
BOBBY	*[makes a move]* Not yet.
TOMMY	*[makes a move]* Checkmate.
BOBBY	*[after making a move]* It's not checkmate until I can't make any more moves.
TOMMY	*[makes a move]* Checkmate!
BOBBY	*[after studying the board]* Darn!

[Tommy stands up and does a little dance.]

TOMMY	I'm bad. I'm bad.
GRANDMA	Tommy, control yourself.
TOMMY	Sorry, Grandma. It's just I never beat Bobby in chess before.
GRANDMA	Well, it's not polite to rub it in.
TOMMY	Yes, ma'am.

[Tommy runs to sofa, picks ups two gloves and a ball, and tosses one glove to Bobby. He prepares to throw the ball.]

TOMMY	For December, it sure is a nice day. Would it be all right if Bobby and I play ball?
ALL 3 ADULTS	Not in the house.
TOMMY	Outside?

GRANDMA	You'd better not. The humans will be back soon.
TOMMY	[pointing to where the dolls will exit later] We'll just be outside the front door.
JIM DANDY	You heard your grandmother, Tommy.
TOMMY	But Dad! What a waste of a perfectly good day.

[Tommy puts gloves on sofa and turns on the television.]

| BOBBY | If we had a TV in my house, I'd watch monster movies all day long. |

[He pretends to turn into a monster and oozes towards his mother and the baby.]

BOBBY	[as monster] I am an alien from the planet Zithra, and I have come to eat your daughter.
MAMA JEAN	[moving away] Stop that, Bobby. You'll frighten your sister.
BOBBY	[as monster] If I cannot eat your daughter, then I will watch a little TV.

[He oozes over to sit beside Tommy.]

JIM DANDY	[holding up papers] These are wonderful plans, Jean. These improvements will make the house beautiful again.
MAMA JEAN	I'm glad you like them.
GRANDMA	I've seen three generations of humans play with this house. A little remodeling is very much in order.
JIM DANDY	If only we could get the humans to do it.
GRANDMA	It'll happen, Jim. You just have to keep thinking those positive thoughts.
JIM DANDY	I've been thinking them, but the humans aren't listening.
GRANDMA	They're listening. They just haven't noticed they're listening.

[SFX — people climbing stairs]

| GRANDMA | Human alert! |

[All the dolls hurry back to the positions they had when the play *began. Tommy has to turn off the TV.]*

GRANDMA   Stiffen up!

[All the dolls turn into dolls. Lights turn off and on rapidly.]

Scene 2: Nancy's bedroom, moments later

KATIE and Nancy enter from SL. Nancy limps to the dollhouse, lifts off roof, and looks inside. Any time a doll talks, he/she does not move and the people do not hear.

NANCY   Katie, look. Tommy finally beat Bobby in chess.

TOMMY   I'm bad. I'm bad.

GRANDMA   Tommy, be quiet!

KATIE   *[talking into dollhouse]* Congratulations Tommy.

              [to Nancy] Thanks for having me over, Nancy. It was fun. Tomorrow you and the Dandys can come to my house.

NANCY   Don't forget. We've got to get some winter coats for the boys.

TOMMY   Shopping? Oh, no!

KATIE   That'd be fun.

MARIE   *[the offstage voice]* Time to go, Katie. Your mother's here.

KATIE   *[shouting towards the voice]* Just a minute.

[Katie now reaches into the dollhouse and marches Bobby out the door. At the same time, inside the dollhouse (SR) Bobby stands and moves stiffly—as if guided by hands—offstage right.]

KATIE   We've got to go, Bobby.

BOBBY   See ya, Tommy.

[As soon as Bobby is offstage, Katie lifts up the doll and talks to him.]

KATIE   *[to doll]* If you behave while we're shopping tomorrow, I'll invite Tommy to spend the night.

TOMMY   Hooray!

MARIE	*[offstage]* Katie, your mother's waiting.
KATIE	*[calling offstage]* I'm coming.
	[to Nancy while putting doll in box) Nancy, what do you think of the new girl, Rosa . . . something?
NANCY	Rosalinda? I like her.
KATIE	Well, she sure talks funny.
NANCY	That's 'cause she's from Mexico. She's just learning English.
KATIE	That's no excuse for her clothes. Maybe we should take her shopping instead of the boys.
TOMMY	Yes!
GRANDMA	Tommy!
NANCY	Good idea. I'll invite her.
KATIE	I was just kidding.
MARIE	*[offstage]* Katie!
KATIE	*[shouting]* I'm on my way, Mrs. Johnson.
	[to herself) Adults.

[Katie returns to dollhouse and marches Mama Jean and Baby Sara out the door. The character Mama Jean gets up and marches offstage the same as Bobby.]

JIM DANDY	Thanks again, Jean.
NANCY	No, we should invite her, not because of her clothes but because she has no friends.
KATIE	I don't know. She seems kind of weird. What will our friends say?
MARIE	*[just offstage]* Katie, now!

[Katie runs to the SL area and looks up, talking to an invisible Marie Johnson just offstage.]

| KATIE | *[holding up Mama Jean doll]* I was just packing, Mrs. Johnson. |

[She runs back, grabs her box and leaves.]

| KATIE | *[to Nancy]* We'll talk about this tomorrow. |

[She exits rapidly with Nancy slowly following.]

TOMMY   Hey, you forgot the roof.

NANCY   *[as if just remembering]* Oops! I forgot the roof.

[She returns to put it in place and then leaves again.]

TOMMY   *[an echo of Katie earlier]* Humans!

[The lights turn on and off rapidly.]

Scene 3: Inside the dollhouse, moments later

GRANDMA   Relax!

[The remaining dolls sigh and turn almost human again. Tommy runs to an invisible window, as if watching the girls leave.]

TOMMY   I can't wait till tomorrow.

GRANDMA   Yes. We've been lucky. Bobby, Jean, and the baby have been our best friends for as long as I can re-member.

[Lights fade to black.]

Scene 4: the school yard, the next day

The dollhouse and table have been removed. The outdoor school bench is in place. (SFX — school bell followed by school kids running out of building.) As the lights come up, Katie and Nancy enter in light coats and carrying their lunch.

KATIE   I'll get the bench.

[She runs ahead. Nancy is slower because of her leg.]

KATIE   *[while opening her bag]* When you come over today, we should have a picnic. We might not have weather like this again until spring.

NANCY   Great idea! We'll pretend it's summer.

[Rosalinda enters and stands off by herself, munching an apple.]

KATIE   I'll get out the barbecue.

NANCY   *[interrupting]* Rosalinda, come join us.

| KATIE | [whispering to Nancy] Not now. We're planning the picnic. |

[Rosalinda does not hear Katie. She hurries over.]

NANCY	Where's your lunch?
ROSALINDA	I am not too hungry.
NANCY	Are you sick?
ROSALINDA	Homesick. I miss Mexico.
KATIE	What's your problem? We've got a lot of great stuff around here.
ROSALINDA	Yes, but I leave my friends, family. Even I miss lunch when *mi granmama* prepare a hot . . . *guiso*, uh, stew. *Es delicioso!*
KATIE	[appalled] Stew? What's wrong with a bologna sandwich? If it's not spicy enough for you, add some mustard.
ROSALINDA	I am sorry. It is not the same.
NANCY	Rosalinda, can you come to my house after school tomorrow? I have a wonderful dollhouse and I'd love to show it to you.
ROSALINDA	[happily] I have a dollhouse too, a big one, ex . . . ex . . . the same as our house in Mexico. Yes. If I get the permission from mi mama, I come tomorrow.
KATIE	[sarcastically to self] Whoopee do!

[Lights fade to black.]

Scene 5: the dollhouse, later that afternoon

To make sure the change to scene 6 goes rapidly, the bench should be gone and the dollhouse and table returned.

When the lights come up, Grandma Dandy is talking on the phone, Jim Dandy is making notes on his house-improvement plans, and Tommy is watching TV while drinking something in a bright silver mug.

| GRANDMA | A cookout? I'd be happy to, Jean. I keep the recipe |

right here in the cupboard. See you soon.

[She hangs up and goes to the cupboard where she notices the missing cup.]

GRANDMA   Tommy!

[Tommy jumps up as if caught doing something wrong.]

GRANDMA   You know you're not supposed to use the silver cup unless Nancy gives it to you. If something should happen . . .

TOMMY   *[relieved not to be in trouble]* Don't worry, Grandma. I'll be careful.

[He sits and watches TV again.]

JIM DANDY   You know, Mother, if this house isn't fixed soon, it'll fall apart.

GRANDMA   You've got to keep thinking those positive thoughts. Why don't you get Nancy to ask for house repairs as a Christmas present.

JIM DANDY   I'll think it. Let's hope she thinks to think it.

[SFX — someone coming up stairs]

GRANDMA   Human alert—stiffen up!

[Grandma Dandy closes cupboard and returns to sofa. Jim Dandy sets down pencil and stands. Tommy turns off TV, guzzles down drink, makes a move for the cupboard, panics, and stuffs the cup inside his shirt. Lights turn off and on rapidly.]

Scene 6: Nancy's bedroom, moments later

Nancy enters as fast as she can. In her rush, she bumps the dollhouse table.

TOMMY   Humanquake!

[All the dolls fall in the same direction, maintaining their stiffness. Nancy removes the roof and looks inside.]

NANCY   Sorry, everyone.

MARIE   *[offstage]* Nancy, where are you going in such a hurry?

NANCY   *[shouting to Mom]* Katie and I are going to pretend it's summer and have a picnic.

MARIE   *[offstage]* In December? You'll catch a cold.

NANCY   *[to Mom]* We'll be careful.

MARIE   *[to self, echoing Katie and Tommy]* Kids!

NANCY   *[to dolls]* Won't it be fun? Grandma Dandy, you can barbecue with your famous hot sauce; Jim Dandy, you can work on your garden; and Tommy, you can play baseball till it's dark.

THE **3** DOLLS TOGETHER   Hooray!

[Lights fade to dark.]

Scene 7: KATIE's front yard, an hour later

When the lights come up, the dollhouse is gone. An upstage door and bush indicate we're in front of KATIE's house. The two girls sit on the ground, their dolls in front of them.

[SFX — a boy's groan]

KATIE   I told you this was a perfect day for a picnic.

NANCY   And Grandma Dandy's barbecued burgers were great!

[SFX — same groan as before]

[Katie picks up Bobby doll.]

KATIE   *[scolding]* I warned you, Bobby. Five was too many!

[She sets doll down.]

NANCY   *[after a pause]* I don't understand you, Katie. How come you're so patient with me and so impatient with Rosalinda?

KATIE   You're my best friend.

NANCY   But Rosalinda needs a friend.

KATIE   When my parents went to Mexico last summer, their luggage was stolen, and when I see her moping all the time, I think she's just feeling sorry for herself.

NANCY   When my leg got hurt in the accident, I was sad all the time, but you tried to make me feel better. Why didn't you think I was just feeling sorry for myself?

KATIE   Your hurt was real. Hers is . . . I don't know . . . fake.

NANCY   How do you fake loneliness?

KATIE   Rosalinda's different. She doesn't deserve to be our friend.

[SFX — another groan. This time it is Grandma Dandy.]
Lights fade to black.

Scene 8: inside the dollhouse, the next afternoon

To make sure the change to scene 9 can be done quickly, KATIE's front door and the bush have been replaced by the dollhouse and table. When the lights come up, the dolls are their humanlike selves. Grandma Dandy is sewing and watching TV while Tommy is marching up and down, obviously upset about something. After a moment, Jim Dandy enters and sets down a briefcase.

JIM DANDY   It's a good thing we had the picnic yesterday. I think it'll snow tonight.

GRANDMA   Oh, good! Just in time for Christmas.

TOMMY   Oh, no! We'll be buried alive.

GRANDMA   What's wrong with you, Tommy? Normally, you love the snow.

TOMMY   [exaggerating] Nothing!

JIM DANDY   That "nothing" meant "something."

TOMMY   Maybe it's the change in the weather.

GRANDMA   Tommy . . . ?

TOMMY   [ashamed] I lost the silver cup.

JIM DANDY   What?

GRANDMA   How?

TOMMY   I took it on the picnic and . . . must have dropped it.

GRANDMA   But that cup was a gift from Nancy's grandmother.

JIM DANDY   This could mean big trouble.

TOMMY   I didn't mean to.

[SFX — girls coming up the steps]

GRANDMA   We'll discuss this later. Human alert! Stiffen up.

[The lights turn off and on rapidly.]

Scene 9: Nancy's bedroom, moments later

*Katie and Nancy enter. Nancy takes the roof off the dollhouse and
Katie marches her dolls into the house. Immediately, Mama Jean,
Baby Sarah, and Bobby walk stiffly into the dollhouse SR.*

KATIE   I got here early Nancy, because Baby Sara caught a cold at the picnic and Mama Jean needs Grandma Dandy's advice.

BOBBY   Hello everybody!

NANCY   *[looking inside]* I'm worried too. Tommy's been acting funny all day. Maybe he caught the same cold.

TOMMY   If I'm sick, it wasn't my fault I lost the cup.

JIM DANDY   Tommy, you weren't sick yesterday.

MARIE   *[offstage]* Nancy, you have company.

KATIE   Darn!

NANCY   *[to Mom]* Send her up, Mom.

     [to Katie] Please be nice to Rosalinda.

KATIE   *[not very convincingly]* I'll try.

[SFX — someone coming up the stairs]

*[Rosalinda enters with a box in her hand. Every comment by KATIE
is barbed.]*

ROSALINDA   Hola, Nancy. Hola, Katie.

KATIE   We say "Hello" in America.

*[Rosalinda is taken aback by this hostility. Nancy has to go to her
and coax her to come over to the dollhouse.]*

NANCY   I'm so glad you could come, Rosalinda. This is the dollhouse I told you about. It belonged first to my grandmother, then my mom, and now me. It needs a little repair, but I think it's the most beautiful house in the world.

ROSALINDA   It is nice. No, it is more than nice. This house has . . . character—the perfect place to raise a family. Now I have a surprise for you. I hope is okay.

[From the box, Rosalinda takes out three dolls, the Valdez family. Nancy is excited. KATIE seems indifferent. After introducing them, Rosalinda marches them into the house, their counterparts doing the same SR. Lolita is the last to enter.]

ROSALINDA   This is Horacio Valdez, his wife Susana, and their daughter Lolita.

NANCY   A pleasure to meet you all. Grandma Dandy will be so happy. She loves meeting new people.

TOMMY   [after spotting Lolita] Oh, no! A girl.

[Rosalinda reaches into the dollhouse. (The audience, of course, cannot see what she is doing.) Suddenly, in the dollhouse (SR), Grandma Dandy stands up and stiffly races offstage right. As soon as the actor is offstage, Rosalinda lifts up the Grandma Dandy doll, hugs it, and races around the room.]

ROSALINDA   This must be Grandma Dandy. I would know her anywhere. She remind me of my own granmama, who still live in Mexico.

KATIE   Careful, Rosalinda. In this country, we try not to squish our grandparents to death.

ROSALINDA   I am sorry. I get too happy.

[She returns the doll to the dollhouse. We see Grandma Dandy enter a bit dizzy, her hair messed, and without her glasses. The girls do not notice.]

MARIE   [offstage] Nancy, bring your friends down for cookies and milk.

NANCY   [to Mom] Thanks, Mom.

[to Rosalinda] Would you like that?

ROSALINDA   Of course. It gives the dolls the chance to get . . . acculated?

KATIE   You mean "acquainted"?

ROSALINDA   Yes.

[The three girls start to leave, KATIE two steps behind.]

KATIE   *[mimicking]* Yesss.

          [to dolls in dollhouse] Watch your valuables.

[They exit SL. The lights turn off and on immediately.]

Scene 10: the dollhouse, moments later

GRANDMA   Relax!

[The Dandys and the Dears relax. The Valdezes do not.]

GRANDMA   What's wrong with Katie?

MAMA JEAN   I don't know. Maybe she caught a cold at the picnic.

GRANDMA   It sounds like a "cold" of the heart. We're going to have to do something.

[Meanwhile the two boys sneak up on the still stiff Valdezes, study them, and then move off by themselves.]

BOBBY   Do you think they're from outerspace?

HORACIO   Relalanse! Que dijo el niño?

[The Mexican dolls relax.]

BOBBY   See! They even speak alien.

TOMMY   *[marching up to Lolita]* Take me to your leader.

BOBBY   Watch it! They may have laser guns in their eyes.

LOLITA   You know, it's not nice to make fun of strangers.

TOMMY   *[pointing to Lolita]* She speaks English!

BOBBY   It may be a trick to win our confidence. Then bam! We're dollburgers!

LOLITA   Please. I have much better taste than to eat you.

GRANDMA   Boys, I'm ashamed. Where are your manners?

[She crosses to the Valdezes and shakes their hands.]

GRANDMA   Mr. and Mrs. Valdez, welcome to our home.

HORACIO   *[to Lolita]* Que dice?

LOLITA   *[to Horacio]* Bienvenidos a su casa.

	[to the others] Thank you. It is a pleasure to meet you, even the scared boys.
TOMMY	Hey, we're not scared of nothing.
GRANDMA	*[correcting his grammar]* Anything.
TOMMY	*[not understanding her correction]* Or anything.
BOBBY	Except alien monsters.
TOMMY	Yeah.
LOLITA	Well, I'm not afraid of certain boys, who behave like alien monsters.
GRANDMA	Well said, Lolita. Please forgive them. They'll grow up eventually. In the meantime, we hope you will come visit us again and again.
BOBBY	*[to Lolita]* I don't get it. How come you speak English and your parents don't?
LOLITA	I was made in Chicago and I watch more TV than they do.
TOMMY	*[to Grandma Dandy]* I told you TV is good for you.
GRANDMA	Not all the time. Not at the expense of your homework.
BOBBY	I wish we had a TV.
MAMA JEAN	Some day, Bobby. We just can't afford one right now.
LOLITA	*[to Bobby]* Maybe for Christmas. If you learn to be nice to strangers, Santa Claus will remember.
GRANDMA	Well, you're not strangers any more.

[SFX — someone coming up the stairs]

GRANDMA	Human alert! Stiffen up.
HORACIO	Seres humanos. Enduranse.

[All the dolls stiffen and freeze. Lights turn off and on immediately.]

Scene 11: Nancy's bedroom, moments later

Rosalinda enters alone.

ROSALINDA   [calling behind her] No thank you, Nancy. I find it al-
               ready.

[Rosalinda talks into the dollhouse before marching her dolls out,
first the parents then Lolita.]

ROSALINDA   I hope you have become friends. When you come
               from so far away, you need good friends as soon as
               possible.

JIM DANDY   Come back soon.

MAMA JEAN   A pleasure to meet you.

BOBBY   [to Lolita] Too bad you're a girl.

[Rosalinda puts her dolls in the box and hurries offstage left.
Lights go off and on immediately.]

                    Scene 12: the dollhouse, moments later

GRANDMA   Relax!

[The dolls do. Suddenly, Tommy notices something.]

TOMMY   Grandma Dandy, where are your glasses?

GRANDMA   They slipped off when Rosalinda picked me up. I
               think they're in the garden just outside.

JIM DANDY   I'll go get them.

[SFX — the girls coming up the stairs]

GRANDMA   No time. Human alert! Stiffen up.

[The dolls return to the positions in which the girls left them and
stiffen. The lights turn off and on immediately.]

                    Scene 13: Nancy's bedroom, moments later

The two girls enter. Nancy goes straight to the dollhouse.

NANCY   Come on, Katie. You know Rosalinda is nice.

KATIE   She's got good manners. That's not the same as be-
               ing nice.

[Nancy notices the glasses are missing. When she moves the

dolls around looking for them, the audience sees the SR dolls
move, one at a time.]

NANCY	Oh dear!
KATIE	What's wrong?
NANCY	Grandma Dandy has lost her glasses.
KATIE	Lost? A doll can't lose anything.
NANCY	They were just here.
KATIE	Maybe you should have searched Rosalinda's pockets before she left.
NANCY	Katie, don't talk like that.
KATIE	You said yourself: "They were just here."

[The cupboard door opens SR.]

NANCY	Oh, no! My grandma's silver cup is missing too.
TOMMY	Uh, oh!
NANCY	I saw it . . . just the other day.
KATIE	Two things in one day. I told you Rosalinda wasn't our kind.
NANCY	There's got to be some other explanation.
KATIE	Why do you think she wanted to come up here by herself? Those good manners were to disguise her plan to steal your things. I'm sorry you had to learn the hard way: foreigners are jealous of everything we have and therefore can never be trusted.

[As she is talking, Katie marches her dolls out of the dollhouse.
At the same time, Mama Jean with baby and Bobby exit SR.]

MAMA JEAN	Call me.
GRANDMA	Yes. We'll have to use all our positive thoughts together.
TOMMY	Positive thoughts, nothing. Katie needs a brain operation.
JIM DANDY	We're got to help Rosalinda.
BOBBY	Even if she is a girl.

[Katie puts her dolls in a box and begins to exits SL. Nancy sits

sadly on the floor.]

NANCY   Don't say anything To Rosalinda yet. Maybe she had a good reason to take my things or there's something we don't know.

KATIE   A crook's a crook. The sooner you tell her to her face the better.

[Katie exits. Nancy just hangs her head.]

MARIE   *[offstage, after a pause]* There's some leftover cookies, Nancy.

NANCY   No thank you, Mom.

MARIE   *[offstage]* Is everything all right?

NANCY   I hope so.

MARIE   *[offstage]* Your new friend has wonderful manners. You can learn a lot from someone who has good manners.

NANCY   Yes, Mom.

TOMMY   *[after a pause]* Hey, don't forget to put on the roof!

GRANDMA   She's not listening, Tommy. Sometimes positive thinking just isn't enough.

[The lights fade to black.]

Scene 14: *inside the dollhouse, an hour later*

When the lights come up, Tommy and Grandma Dandy are marching back and forth obviously worried. Suddenly, Tommy stops and turns.

TOMMY   Frankly, I'm disappointed in Nancy's behavior.

GRANDMA   Nancy's? What about yours?

TOMMY   Mine? I didn't do nothing!

GRANDMA   *[correcting]* "Anything"!

TOMMY   Anything . . . to Rosalinda.

GRANDMA   I'm talking about the way you treated Lolita.

TOMMY   Lolita? But she's a girl!

GRANDMA   She was a guest in this house.

TOMMY   But girls don't know noth . . . anything about foot-
            ball, baseball, basketball—the important stuff.

GRANDMA   How do you know? Did you ask her? You act like you
            were born in the thirties.

TOMMY   I was.

GRANDMA   Thomas Dandy, that is no excuse for rudeness.

[Enter Jim Dandy, glasses in hand.]

JIM DANDY   I found them, right where you said they'd be. Now,
            where do we put them so Nancy can find them.

TOMMY   On top of the TV.

GRANDMA   No, Nancy would have seen them before.

JIM DANDY   How about the kitchen?

GRANDMA   But we weren't in the kitchen . . . I've got it!
            Humanquakes! Come here.

[The three huddle together, Grandma Dandy giving instructions
the audience cannot hear. Together they push the sofa upstage
and set the glasses where the sofa was. Tommy then runs to the
invisible window and watches for a few seconds.]

[SFX — someone coming up the stairs]

GRANDMA   Remember: everyone think "bump." Human Alert!
            Stiffen up!

[The dolls do. Nancy enters, still upset. She approaches the
dollhouse but does not look inside.]

NANCY   [hitting table lightly] I just don't believe it.

GRANDMA   Now.

[The three dolls fall over, creating just enough noise to alert
Nancy. When she looks inside, she will see what the audience
sees SR. The three dolls have fallen in such a way that they all
point to the glasses.]

NANCY   I didn't hit the table that hard. I guess this old house
            is getting a bit shaky . . . The glasses! Oh, Grandma
            Dandy, I am so happy. This means Rosalinda didn't
            steal them! Now if I can only figure out what hap-

pened to the silver cup.

GRANDMA   And get it back!

TOMMY   Before the whole world gets into trouble.

JIM DANDY   The whole world?

TOMMY   Yeah. Me!

[Lights fade to black.]

Scene 15: the school yard, lunch time, the next Monday

The dollhouse and table have been removed. When the lights come up, the two girls are eating lunch in their winter coats on the bench.

NANCY   . . . so the glasses were under the sofa all along. They must have fallen off when . . .

KATIE   [interrupting] That still doesn't explain what happened to the silver cup. Remember, we never had these kinds of problems before Miss Sourface came along.

[Rosalinda enters from SL, bag lunch in hand. When she sees Katie, she waves, but Katie pretends not to see her. Nancy never does notice Rosalinda in this scene.]

NANCY   Maybe if we're extra nice, she'll give it back.

KATIE   We don't need her. When you come over today, we'll have a great time all by ourselves.

[Rosalinda hears this last part, realizes she is not wanted, and leaves.]

NANCY   Maybe her move here was like my accident, making her do things she normally wouldn't. When my leg . . .

KATIE   Why do you want to defend a thief? We tried to be her friend but she took advantage. What would your grandmother say if she found out?

NANCY   She might say we should forgive Rosalinda.

KATIE   Or she might say we were fools to trust a stranger and not take better care of her prized silver cup.

[Lights fade to black.]

Scene 16: Nancy's bedroom, a few days later

The bench is gone; the dollhouse and table are back. All the actor dolls are downstage right in a half circle, in front of the audience. A bright light is on the floor in front of them giving the lighting effect of a fire. When the other lights come up, the girls are look-ing into the unroofed dollhouse.

NANCY   The best part of winter is a fire in the fireplace.

KATIE   With friends.

NANCY   How do you think the Valdezes are doing?

KATIE   I thought we agreed not to talk about Rosalinda any more.

NANCY   But this kind of winter is new to them.

KATIE   I'll tell you what: The day Rosalinda returns your sil-ver cup and apologizes we'll invite her back as a friend. Until then, let's forget her.

MARIE   *[offstage]* Nancy, come down here please. I have a surprise for you.

KATIE   Hey, maybe your dad's going to fix the dollhouse, as a Christmas present.

NANCY   I doubt it. Dad said dollhouse repair is a special skill and expensive.

GRANDMA   Good thinking, Jim.

JIM DANDY Thank you.

[The two exit SL. The lights turn off and on rapidly.]

Scene 17: the dollhouse, moments later

Throughout this scene, the dolls enjoy the warmth of the fire.

GRANDMA   Relax!

[They do.]

MAMA JEAN   Poor Rosalinda.

JIM DANDY   And the Valdezes!

GRANDMA   We'll never see them again unless we somehow get the silver cup back.

TOMMY   [starting to leave] That settles it. Cold or no cold, I'll get it myself.

MAMA JEAN   How?

JIM DANDY   None of us knows the way.

GRANDMA   For three generations I've traveled in a box, a suitcase, or a little girl's deep pockets.

TOMMY   But it can't be that far away.

JIM DANDY   It isn't—if you know where you're going.

[SFX — the two girls coming up the stairs]

GRANDMA   Human alert! Stiffen up.

[The dolls do. The lights turn off and on rapidly.]

                    Scene 18: Nancy's bedroom, moments later

NANCY   [still offstage] Thank you, Mom. Thank you, thank you, thank you!

KATIE   [entering] It's wonderful, and just in time for Christmas.

[The two girls hurry to the dollhouse. The audience has no idea why they are so happy until they see Santa Claus march stiffly into the SR living room.]

NANCY   [peering into the dollhouse] Grandma Dandy, please introduce everyone while Katie and I have lunch.

               [to Katie] Then we'll go over to your house and ask your mom if you can spend the night.

[The two girls exit SL. The lights turn off and on rapidly.]

Scene 19: the dollhouse, moments later

GRANDMA   Relax.

[The dolls do. Then Bobby runs over to inspect Santa the way he did the Valdezes earlier.]

BOBBY   Run for your lives! It's a space alien!

MAMA JEAN   Bobby, it's Santa Claus!

BOBBY   *[pointing]* No, it's a long-haired, red-suited, big-bel-lied alien.

EVERYONE   That's Santa Claus!

BOBBY   *[approaching Santa cautiously]* Prove to me you're not an alien.

SANTA CLAUS   Ho, ho, ho!

BOBBY   *[to others]* Space talk.

TOMMY   Santa talk. I've seen it on TV.

BOBBY   I'm not convinced.

SANTA CLAUS   Do you want more proof, Bobby?

BOBBY   How'd you know my name?

SANTA CLAUS   According to my records, you are often naughty and not nice to strangers.

[For a moment, Bobby is too shocked to speak. Then he turns, smiles, and hugs Santa.]

BOBBY   Santa Claus!

SANTA CLAUS   Stop slobbering, Bobby. You're worse than the rein-deer.

TOMMY   Hey, everybody, I've got an idea how to get the silver cup back.

EVERYONE   How?

TOMMY   Santa, as a world traveler, you know this neighbor-hood like the back of your hand, right?

SANTA CLAUS   *[pointing to head]* It's all up here in the sawdust.

TOMMY   So you know the way to Katie's house.

SANTA CLAUS   Two blocks south, then east.

TOMMY   Come on, everyone. Let's go find the silver cup.

[Everyone cheers—except Santa.]

SANTA CLAUS   Just a minute. I'm not in the lost and found business. Maybe you should talk to the Tooth Fairy.

JIM DANDY   But, Santa, this is very important!

MAMA JEAN   Worth at least a couple hundred Christmas wishes!

TOMMY   World peace and international understanding are at stake!

GRANDMA   And two girls might lose a valuable friend!

SANTA CLAUS   Hm-m-m.

EVERYONE   Please?

SANTA CLAUS   There's the chance someone will see us.

[All the dolls say things like "We'll be careful," etc.]

SANTA CLAUS   It's very cold this time of year.

[The dolls answer "No Problem," "We're tough," etc.]

SANTA CLAUS   All right, we'll do it.

[The dolls cheer.]

SANTA CLAUS   Next spring, when it's warmer.

EVERYONE   What?

SANTA CLAUS   Just kidding. Ho, ho, ho!

GRANDMA   Get your coats. We're on our way.

[The lights fade to black.]

Scene 20: outdoors, minutes later

While the lights are out and coats are put on, the stage is cleared. When the lights come up, the dolls are entering the audience on a U-shaped journey that will get them to KATIE's house. The order is Santa, Tommy, Bobby, Mama Jean (and baby), Grandma Dandy, and Jim Dandy.

SANTA CLAUS   *[pointing]* We'll turn up there.

TOMMY   This world of the humans is really weird.

BOBBY   Maybe they are the real aliens.

MAMA JEAN   That would explain Katie's strange behavior lately.

GRANDMA   [pointing to audience] Look at that grass. We would need a machete to cut it.

JIM DANDY   At least it's not snowing.

[SFX — car passing by loudly]

BOBBY   A spaceship! Everyone duck!

[They do.]

JIM DANDY   Bobby, that was just a human car.

BOBBY   Well, it sounded like a spaceship.

SANTA CLAUS   Turn again here. We're almost there.

[Depending on the stage and size of audience, the actor/dolls may need to add a few lines about the giant world of humans in order to get back to the stage. When they get there, the lights do not change.]

Scene 21: KATIE's front yard, moments later

GRANDMA   Okay, everyone, spread out. That cup has got to be around here someplace.

[The dolls crisscross back and forth looking for the silver cup.]

JIM DANDY   Anybody find anything?

BOBBY   [reaching down] Here's a French fry. That means we're close.

MAMA JEAN   Bobby Dear, throw that away now!

[Off to one side, Tommy finds a large disc with four holes in it.]

TOMMY   Grandma, what's this?

GRANDMA   It's a human button, to hold clothes in place.

BOBBY   [shouting] Careful, everyone. An alien's about to lose its pants.

SANTA CLAUS   Ho, ho, ho!

MAMA JEAN   [lifting up cup found just offstage] Is this it?

[Tommy runs over and hugs it like an old friend.]

TOMMY   Oh, I'll never let you out of my sight again.

JIM DANDY   What's that noise?

[SFX — a boom, boom, boom—a giant's footsteps]

BOBBY   Human alert! Stiffen up.

[Bobby stiffens, but Grandma Dandy runs over and shakes him.]

GRANDMA   No, no, no! If it's the girls, they mustn't find us here. Quick, everyone—hide in the grass before they see us.

[There is a general confusion with dolls running into each other, running in circles, tripping, etc. At one point, Tommy drops the cup and it goes offstage left.]

TOMMY   The cup!

GRANDMA   Too late. We'll get it when the humans leave.

[The group pulls Tommy into the audience where they hide. Lights turn off and on.]

Scene 22: in front of KATIE's house, moments later

The door and bush are returned as in Scene 7. Katie and Nancy enter from SR.

KATIE   I'll just check with my mom, grab my toothbrush, and we can go.

NANCY   I'll wait here.

[Suddenly Rosalinda appears SR. She looks cold and sad.]

ROSALINDA   I am sorry to bother you, but I wish to talk.

KATIE   [heading for the front door] We're busy right now.

ROSALINDA   I thought we were being friends. Now you don't speak to me. Why?

KATIE   We don't have to explain anything.

ROSALINDA   Did I say something? Nancy, we shared . . .

KATIE   [interrupting] That's right: we shared. You stole.

ROSALINDA   What?

KATIE   You should know in this country you can't just steal something and get away with it.

ROSALINDA   I don't understand. Steal what?

KATIE   The day you came to Nancy's house, a valuable silver cup disappeared.

ROSALINDA   You mean . . . a trophy?

KATIE   Don't play innocent. It was a doll's cup and you know it.

[The girls have been moving as they talk. Now Rosalinda is in a position to spot the silver cup just offstage.]

ROSALINDA   A doll's cup? You mean like this?

[She retrieves the cup and hands it to Nancy.]

NANCY   This is it! My silver cup! Oh, Rosalinda, I am so sorry.

KATIE   How did it get here? I don't understand.

NANCY   I think I do. Katie, you were the one who convinced me Rosalinda took it. You warned me over and over that she could not be trusted.

KATIE   What? Do you think I stole it?

NANCY   You wanted me to be angry with Rosalinda and you would do anything to prove she was unworthy.

KATIE   No, I never . . .

ROSALINDA   [interceding] Wait, Nancy. Think about it: If someone steal you cup, they hide it, not throw it in the grass here. Katie is your best friend for years. She would not steal it ever. You know that.

NANCY   You're defending her?

KATIE   You're defending me?

ROSALINDA   I defend two people I think are almost my friends. They would not hurt each other. Never. Think again. Did you ever play here with the dolls in the grass?

KATIE AND NANCY   [together] The picnic!

NANCY   I must have accidentally brought the cup, then dropped it.

KATIE   [moving from place to place] This is where we had the barbecue. And this is where Bobby ate many imaginary hamburgers and French fries.

NANCY   I'm sorry, Katie. I'm even more sorry, Rosalinda.

ROSALINDA   A friend never hurts another friend on purpose, but if by accident they do, they must forgive each other quickly. That is the rule.

KATIE   Did you learn that in Mexico?

ROSALINDA   Yes, but it is true everywhere.

[The three girls hug for a moment.]

KATIE   Rosalinda, we're spending the night at Nancy's. Do you think you could come?

ROSALINDA   If Nancy's mother calls mi mama, I think yes.

KATIE   And could you show us your Mexican dollhouse?

ROSALINDA   The perfect time is now. Come. I show you.

NANCY   And tell us more about your grandmama. Grandma Dandy says good kids are the result of good grand-parents.

GRANDMA   I have never been wrong about that.

[The three head offstage left. The lights turn off and on. The bush and door are removed.]

Scene 23: in front of Katie's house, moments later

MAMA JEAN   I am so proud of Rosalinda.

TOMMY   Rosalinda? What about me? I'm the hero. If I hadn't dropped the cup, the girls might never have become friends.

JIM DANDY   If you hadn't dropped the cup, all this confusion could have been avoided.

TOMMY   All right, then I'm the almost hero.

             [starts to dance] I'm bad. I'm bad.

GRANDMA   If grandparents deserve the credit for their grand-children's behavior, I'll soon be moving from the Dandy home to a cuckoo clock.

JIM DANDY   We'd better get back before the girls return.

SANTA CLAUS   Follow me.

[The dolls pass through the audience, traveling in the opposite direction of before.]

BOBBY   I'm very happy, Mother.

MAMA JEAN   Why Bobby?

BOBBY   Because the human beings have turned out to be friendly aliens.

GRANDMA   We're going to have to get the Valdezes something for Christmas, something that will make them feel more at home here.

JIM DANDY   How? We haven't any money?

GRANDMA   If we all think the right thoughts, Nancy and Katie will think them too—all by themselves. Well, almost all by themselves. We'll talk more about it when we get home.

[As the dolls approach the stage, the lights fade to black.]

Scene 24: the Dandy dollhouse, one week later

The furniture is back on SR and the dollhouse is on its table SL. When the lights come up, all the adult dolls are there. They have just finished eating and have plates on their laps or at the dining table.

GRANDMA   *[to Valdezes]* We are so glad to have you back.

HORACIO   It is our pleasure.

SUSANA   The dinner was delicious.

MAMA JEAN   I'm impressed how quickly you've learned English.

SUSANA   Still much to learn.

SANTA CLAUS   Cuando es necesano, puedo servir como interprete.

JIM DANDY   Santa, I didn't know you could speak Spanish.

SANTA CLAUS   A world traveler must know many languages.

JIM DANDY   What will you do after Christmas?

SANTA CLAUS   *[surprised by the question]* Change my clothes.

[The three doll children enter. The boys are obviously depressed. Tommy carries a soccer ball.]

GRANDMA   What's wrong? Was somebody hurt?

BOBBY   We thought we'd teach Lolita a soccer lesson . . .

TOMMY   . . . but she taught us.

               [puts ball on floor and prepares to kick it] She hit a goal from the corner just like . . .

ALL ADULTS   Not in the house!

[Tommy sets the ball on the sofa and goes to the cupboard to get the silver cup.]

GRANDMA   Tommy . . .

TOMMY   Don't worry. I've learned my lesson.

LOLITA   Don't feel badly, Bobby. In my country, we play *futbal*, ah, soccer, everyday. We also play baseball, but I am not very good. Maybe you teach me baseball and I'll teach you soccer.

BOBBY   It's a deal.

[SFX — footsteps coming up the stairs.]

GRANDMA   Human alert! Stiffen up.

[The dolls hurry to their places and freeze. Tommy again panics and stuffs the cup in his shirt. The lights blink off and on.]

Scene 25: Nancy's room, moments later

Katie and Nancy enter.

KATIE   Where'd Rosalinda go?

NANCY   She said she had to get something.

[Enter Rosalinda, carrying two wrapped boxes.]

ROSALINDA   I have a Christmas surprise for you.

NANCY   You shouldn't have. We didn't get you nothing.

GRANDMA   Anything!

NANCY   I mean "anything."

ROSALINDA   Your gift to me is . . . if you like it. Katie, first for you.

[She gives Katie the bigger box. She opens it and pulls out a doll-size TV.]

KATIE   Oh, it's a TV set for my dollhouse.

BOBBY   Hooray!

KATIE   It's just what the Dears wanted.

ROSALINDA   And now, Nancy, for you.

[She hands Nancy a shoebox. Inside, there's a hammer.]

NANCY   *[puzzled]* A hammer? Thanks, but what . . . ?

ROSALINDA   *[laughing]* It is not for you. It is for Grandma Dandy, Jim Dandy, and Tommy. My father, his hobby is *carpentaria*—carpentry. He say he will fix this old house to look like new.

JIM DANDY   *[echoing Tommy]* I'm bad. I'm bad.

GRANDMA   The power of Dandy thinking!

ROSALINDA   While the house is in repair, the Dandys can stay with the Valdez family. It will be like a Mexican vacation.

THE 3 DANDYS Hooray!

[Tommy suddenly remembers the cup and moves slowly, stiffly, towards the cupboard.]

GRANDMA   Tommy, be still!

TOMMY   Can't.

GRANDMA   *[after a short pause]* Girls, don't forget Rosalinda's gift.

KATIE   *[to Nancy]* Oh, we almost forgot! Nancy, get Rosalinda her gift.

ROSALINDA   But you say you don't have nothing.

GRANDMA   *[correcting]* Anything!

ROSALINDA   Anything.

NANCY   It's not for you. It's for the Valdezes.

[Nancy hands Rosalinda a small package. While she opens it, Tommy again moves slowly towards the cupboard.]

ROSALINDA   It's a tiny piñata. Where did you find it? The Valdezes will be so happy.

KATIE   You use it at Christmas, right? I looked it up.

NANCY   It's from Santa . . . and the others.

[Rosalinda looks inside the dollhouse. Tommy freezes.]

ROSALINDA   Thank you, Santa.

SANTA CLAUS   De nada.

[When Rosalinda turns back to her friends, Tommy moves again.
He is almost there.]

ROSALINDA   And thank you, too. I have not been so happy since
Mexico.

[The three embrace and start jumping up and down.]

ALL DOLLS   Humanquake!

[They bounce around stiffly and finally fall down on top of each
other. Tommy drops the cup and it bounces wherever.]

GRANDMA   Here we go again.

MARIE   [offstage] Calm down up there! Kids!

THE THREE GIRLS   Adults!

ALL DOLLS   Humans!

[The three girls look inside the dollhouse.]

KATIE   Well, everyone seems to be getting along.

NANCY   They're having as much fun as us.

ROSALINDA   I speak for the Valdezes: I think it is going to be a
great new year.

THE END

The Clark Campaign

A radio play

THE DANGER OF WRITING AND PRODUCING ANY HISTORY PLAY is oversimplification. Since we know how the big event turned out, we tend to make the choices clear and provide our heroes with proper motivation. We want the good guys to be rewarded and the bad guys to be punished for not recognizing history for what it would become.

The challenge then is to recreate the dilemmas, doubt, and controversy that bond the past with the present. The most corrupt had their "good reasons," just as the most noble had their petty complaints. Of course, every history play is an interpretation (as opposed to a reproduction), but the details will give it second life. Your audience may admire the generals, but it will worry about the soldiers, and an important victory may reflect what the front line had for breakfast as much as clever battle strategy. You will know you are on the right track when you sometimes confuse the good guys with the bad.

For example, the outcome of the Battle of Fort Sackville was in doubt from the moment Colonel Clark organized his Kentucky troops until Lieutenant Governor Hamilton raised the white flag. Clark's trip was a calculated gamble, and if the journey had been delayed just one more day or had Hamilton been less concerned for his men and more concerned with the disgrace that accompanies surrender, Colonel Clark's campaign would be important only in British and Canadian history books. The same qualities that made Colonel Clark such a superb military leader would make him a lousy next-door neighbor.

The Battle of Fort Sackville was Colonel Clark's finest hour, in part because he believed it was just the beginning. He envisioned smashing victories at Fort Detroit and a grateful free America that would reward his service and sacrifice.

He never made it to Fort Detroit, and the struggling Confederation of American States never authorized the repayment of Clark's expenses. The British lost territory; Colonel Clark lost his wealth and youth. As the British felt deceived that Clark's mighty army was a hoax, Clark felt betrayed that the nation's gratitude ended with a simple thank you.

The advantages of producing a radio play are obvious. Expenses are limited to the cost of a few sound effects, and blocking (positioning of performers on stage) is minimal. But for this same reason, the text of the play becomes more important. The actors must concentrate on the meaning (subtext) of each sentence and speak with an energy that invites listeners to visualize what is happening in their heads. Remember, the British are frightened, the Americans feel vulnerable, and the reporters pride themselves on being professional.

Although Clark's contribution was ignored during his lifetime, an enthusiastic production will honor his memory with silent applause.

This play was first produced at Royerton Elementary School in Muncie, Indiana, and broadcast of WWDS Radio on February 25, 1980.

Characters

Fill in student performer's name below and use the name as designated by character and by blanks throughout the play.

Announcer _____
Anchorwoman _____
Student Reporters:
Reporter A _____
Reporter B _____
Reporter C _____
Reporter D _____
Reporter E _____
Reporter F _____
American Soldiers:
Soldier 1 _____
Soldier 2 _____
Soldier 3 _____

Soldier 4   _____
British soldier   _____
Vincennes woman 1   _____
Vincennes woman 2   _____
Vincennes woman 3   _____
Lieutenant Governor Henry Hamilton   _____
Major Joseph Bowman   _____
Colonel George Rogers Clark   _____
Soldiers in background   _____
Governor Patrick Henry   _____

The Clark Campaign
February 25, 1779
The Battle of Fort Sackville

ANNOUNCER   Ladies and gentlemen, we interrupt your regular classroom programming to bring you the following special news feature: The Clark Campaign: February 25, 1779; the Battle of Fort Sackville.

[SFX — Typewriter, standard news programming background noise]

ANNOUNCER   And now from campaign headquarters in Vincennes, north of Kentucky, here is ——— (Anchorwoman).

ANCHORWOMAN Good morning. Yesterday afternoon, Colonel George Rogers Clark surrounded the British held Fort Sackville in Vincennes and demanded immediate surrender. The British commander, Lieutenant Governor Henry Hamilton refused. After several hours of fighting, Hamilton asked Clark for a three day truce. Clark has denied that request, leaving Hamilton the final choice of whether to surrender or fight. His decision could have a major effect on the outcome of the American Revolution. Should Hamilton fight and win, the already demoralized American troops in the east would find themselves being attacked on yet a third front. It could very well mean the end of the American dream of independence. To better understand the situation, I switch you now to ——— (Reporter A) on the American front lines just outside the fort.

[SFX — *cannon shot*]

REPORTER A ——— (Anchorwoman), I'm standing here with the French and American sharpshooters that Colonel Clark had sent forward early yesterday afternoon.

[SFX — *cannon*] Despite being only fifteen yards from the fort, I'm actually in less danger than the other soldiers farther back. These sharpshooters keep the British away from the walls and the cannons have no choice but to shoot over our heads.

[SFX — *cannon*] Excuse me, soldier. Where are you from?

SOLDIER 1 Me? I'm from Virginia; live in the Kentucky region.

REPORTER A Tell us something about the trip to get here.

SOLDIER 1 Swum more than I walked, thought my feet would web. Sixteen days. Sometimes up to our necks in ice water. I'll tell you what I'm going to do. The moment we capture them British, I'm going to find myself a nice, dry bed, lay down and get rightfully sick for about a month.

[SFX — *cannon*]

REPORTER A You must be a great believer in the Revolution.

SOLDIER 1 The Revolution be hanged! I believe in my family. That Mr. Hamilton — ol' "Hair-Buyer" — is paying the Indians to sharpen their knives on our heads. As soon as we stop him, I'm going home.

ANCHORWOMAN ——— (Reporter A), excuse me for interrupting, but Colonel Clark has just come out of a meeting and is standing with reporter ——— (Reporter B). Go ahead, ——— (Reporter B).

[SFX — *milling crowd*]

REPORTER B	Colonel Clark, a lot of our listeners are worried about the way the Revolution is going so far. Could you say anything which might encourage them?
COL. CLARK	Freedom is never free.
REPORTER B	Are you surprised you made it here through the flood waters and cold temperatures?
COL. CLARK	I would have bee surprised had anyone else done it.
REPORTER B	Does that mean you expect the British to surrender?
COL. CLARK	We are preparing ourselves for a fight.
REPORTER B	But most of your men are sick. You wouldn't stand a chance.
COL. CLARK	Hamilton didn't think we stood a chance to get here.
REPORTER B	Excuse me, Colonel, but there are rumors that your men massacred a group of Indian scalp-hunters in front of the fort this morning. Would you care to comment on that?
COL. CLARK	No, I wouldn't.
	[leaves] Where's Major Bowman? I want the two French units to . . .
ANCHORWOMAN	Thank you, ——— (Reporter B). We've heard from the Americans. Let's go inside the fort now and find out what the British are thinking. ——— (Reporter C), can you hear me?
REPORTER C	This is ——— (Reporter C), outside Governor Hamilton's office. He has just called an emergency meeting for all his officers.
ANCHORWOMAN	Is there any chance you could get into the room? It would be interesting to overhear the conversation.
REPORTER C	The doors are closed to all but officers. I think that's an indication of just how desperate Hamilton finds the crisis.
ANCHORWOMAN	Have you talked to any of the British soldiers to get their reactions?
REPORTER C	They're pretty upset with what they witnessed this morning. They're convinced Colonel Clark means to

cut them up the same way he did the Indians.

[turns to soldier] Excuse me, soldier. Do you think Lieutenant Governor Hamilton will fight?

BRITISH SOLDIER   I don't know. I don't know what to think.

REPORTER C   Are you prepared to fight?

BRITISH SOLDIER   You mean are we prepared to die? If we fight, we'll be butchered by the Americans; and if we surrender, we'll go to prison and starve to death. If the Americans don't have the supplies to fight a war, how can they feed the prisoners?

REPORTER C   Would you run if you could?

BRITISH SOLDIER   I'd go home if I could. Let the Americans and Indians have this land. They deserve it; they deserve each other. This isn't our fight; we should be back in England.

ANCHORWOMAN   ——— (Reporter C), I'm going to cut in here because ——— (Reporter D) has just gotten ahold of Governor Patrick Henry in Richmond, Virginia. We're listening, ——— (Reporter D).

REPORTER D   Governor, what chances do you give Colonel Clark of capturing Fort Sackville?

GOV. HENRY   What chances do you give the British of sleeping the next six months?

REPORTER D   Have you heard from him?

GOV. HENRY   Only that he's left on a desperate attempt to capture the fort.

REPORTER D   Then you don't think he has a chance?

GOV. HENRY   Clark's a remarkable man, but he doesn't have the men or supplies. In addition, this is the middle of winter, rivers are overflowing; the temperature is close to freezing. I wish I could have been of some help but the war expenses here. They just keep going up and up. Excuse me, but I have local emergencies to attend to.

ANCHORWOMAN   Thank you, ——— (Reporter D). ——— (Reporter

C), let us know the moment Hamilton comes out of his meeting. In the meantime, let's go down into the village of Vincennes, and find out what the French say about all of this. ——— (Reporter E)? ——— (Reporter E), are you there?

REPORTER E   I'm here all right, some three hundred yards from the fort, talking with some of the women who call Vincennes home.

VINCENNES WOMAN 1   *Called* Vincennes home.

VINCENNES WOMAN 2   That's right. The British fight the Americans but so far the only casualties have been our homes.

VINCENNES WOMAN 3   So what have we done that the British cannons shoot at us?

[SFX — *cannon followed by whistles and explosion.*]

REPORTER E   Does that mean you people hope the Americans will win?

VINCENNES WOMAN 1   Father Gibault says the Americans make the best rulers, but who knows? We wait. If the British win, it's better we keep our mouths shut.

REPORTER E   Where are your husbands? Indoors?

VINCENNES WOMAN 3   Indoors is too dangerous.

[SFX — *cannon followed by whistles and explosion.*]

VINCENNES WOMAN 2   My husband fights with the Americans.

VINCENNES WOMAN 3   My husband fights for no one.

VINCENNES WOMAN 1   My husband is rebuilding our house and swearing bullets at the British.

ANCHORWOMAN   That's fine, ——— (Reporter E). I switch you now to ——— (Reporter F) who is talking with Major Bowman, Colonel Clark's second in command and best friend. I believe he is talking with some of the sick men.

MAJOR BOWMAN   [*talking to soldier*] We need you, soldier, not just to get better but to pull a trigger. Can we count on you?

REPORTER F   Excuse me, Major Bowman?

MAJOR BOWMAN [*still paying no attention to reporter*] You didn't suffer so much to get here just to lie down on us, did you? [*turning to reporter*] Yes, what is it?

[*SFX — sounds of sick men in background*]

REPORTER F Could you tell us about that trip?

MAJOR BOWMAN Impossible.

REPORTER F I beg your pardon.

MAJOR BOWMAN Impossible. It couldn't have been done by anyone else but Clark. He kept the troops moving when everyone would have sooner laid down and died. We hiked and slept wet, didn't eat a decent meal the last six days.

REPORTER F I can see you have a great deal of faith in the man. You must be predicting an easy victory.

MAJOR BOWMAN Come over here; I'd rather the others didn't hear this.

[*SFX — walking, with sick men in background*]

MAJOR BOWMAN If the British fight, we don't stand a chance. They're fresh; we're exhausted. They have cannons; we have muskets.

REPORTER F Then how can Colonel Clark act so confident?

MAJOR BOWMAN Bluff.

REPORTER F Bluff?

MAJOR BOWMAN For the men, for the British, for everyone. Even his plan of attack is a bluff.

REPORTER F I don't understand.

MAJOR BOWMAN Of our 170 men, only a handful were strong enough to carry the troop banners, so Colonel Clark had them parade past that hill over there many times so the British would think we had a huge army of able-bodied men. Then he sent these same men to the front line outside the fort. The first line is the only line, except the British don't know that.

REPORTER F The plan sounds pretty risky.

MAJOR BOWMAN   If it works, Clark will be a hero. If if doesn't, well, we would have lost anyway.

REPORTER C   Excuse me, ——— (Reporter F), but I was told to interrupt the moment Hamilton dismissed his officers.

[SFX — *men rushing around to do urgent business.*]

REPORTER C   [*fighting through the crowd*] Governor Hamilton? Governor Hamilton? Have you come to any decision?

GOV. HAMILTON   I'd rather not say until I've talked to my troops.

REPORTER C   Can you tell us what was discussed in the meeting?

GOV. HAMILTON   We were considering the odds. They have a thousand men to our 150, they are all excellent riflemen, and this Clark must be a superb organizer to have brought so many men without greater difficulty.

REPORTER C   It doesn't look very good.

GOV. HAMILTON   We could try to hold out until reinforcements arrive but should Clark's men break through, I dread to think what his men would do to mine. It's either surrender or prepare ourselves for an awfully bloody battle. [*leaving*] Is there any word from . . . ?

ANCHORWOMAN   We should know Hamilton's decision any minute now. In the meantime, ——— (Reporter F), how are the men responding to all this pressure? We left you before you could conclude your interview with Major Bowman.

REPORTER F   After Major Bowman left, many started complaining. They wonder if he hasn't gone too far this time, expects too much. He got them here, but many are too weak to lift their guns, let alone aim and fire. Listen . . .

SOLDIER 2   Clark's crazy. He can't really expect us to fight.

SOLDIER 3   We need time to rest.

SOLDIER 2   I never expected it to be this bad. None of us would have come if we knew it was going to be like this.

SOLDIER 4   Trust Clark, will ya? Or would you rather be a British prisoner?

SOLDIER 3	I'd rather be alive.
SOLDIER 4	No one has died yet, have they?
SOLDIER 2	This afternoon Clark plans to make up for lost time.
SOLDIER 4	And I say trust him. If we have gone this long, it seems silly to give up on him now.
SOLDIER 3	Look! The fort! They're raising the white flag!

[SFX — loud cheering]

REPORTER F It's true ——— (Anchorwoman)! The front gates of the fort are opening and Hamilton is marching out. I don't see Clark . . . Wait, there he is! He's walking forward to accept Hamilton's sword.

[SFX — drum beat and then more cheering]

GOV. HAMILTON But sir, where are your troops?

COL. CLARK Don't worry Governor. You were outmanned ten-to-one because my men are worth ten of anyone else's.

[SFX — more loud cheering]

ANCHORWOMAN ——— (Reporter C) or ——— (Reporter F), try to get a statement from Clark. How does he expect this to change the course of the Revolution? Have the British finally been stopped in the West?

REPORTER F Colonel Clark, tell us the significance of this victory.

COL. CLARK *[Ignoring the reporter]* Take the sick inside, Major Bowman. I want the officers locked up and the British soldiers at attention in the courtyard.

REPORTER F Congratulations, Colonel Clark. What are your plans now?

COL. CLARK Detroit. End the Indian menace and the threat of another British attack. But I don't know. We need supplies, the men need rest; but a month from now might be too late. *[leaving]* I want to talk to the townspeople too . . .

ANCHORWOMAN ——— (Reporter F), you're up there close, what are your impressions of the man?

REPORTER F It's hard to say. If he hadn't brought his men

through so much, I'd say he was a crackpot. If he hadn't outsmarted the British, I'd have called him a fool. He risked the life of every man under his command, but lost no one. Let's put it this way: if Washington had a dozen more like him, the war would be over in a month, one way or another.

ANCHORWOMAN Thank you, ——— (Reporter F). And that's the way it is February 25, 1779, the first day of rest for 170 American soldiers after the capture of Fort Sackville this morning.

[SFX — *standard news programming background noise*]

ANNOUNCER We now return you to your regular classroom programming.

THE END